Dragon Lore™
The Official Strategy Guide

NOW AVAILABLE FROM PRIMA

Computer Game Books

The 7th Guest: The Official Strategy Guide
Aces Over Europe: The Official Strategy Guide
Aegis: Guardian of the Fleet—The Official Strategy Guide
Betrayal at Krondor: The Official Strategy Guide
CD-ROM Games Secrets, Volume 1
Computer Adventure Games Secrets
DOOM Battlebook
DOOM II: The Official Strategy Guide
Dracula Unleashed: The Official Strategy Guide & Novel
Front Page Sports Baseball '94: The Official Playbook
Harpoon II: The Official Strategy Guide
Master of Orion: The Official Strategy Guide
Microsoft Flight Simulator: The Official Strategy Guide
Microsoft Golf: The Official Strategy Guide
Microsoft Space Simulator: The Official Strategy Guide
Might and Magic Compendium: The Authorized Strategy Guide for Games I, II, III, and IV
Myst: The Official Strategy Guide
Outpost: The Official Strategy Guide
Pagan: Ultima VIII—The Ultimate Strategy Guide
Panzer General: The Official Strategy Guide
Prince of Persia: The Official Strategy Guide
Quest for Glory: The Authorized Strategy Guide
Rebel Assault: The Official Insider's Guide
Return to Zork Adventurer's Guide
Shadow of the Comet: The Official Strategy Guide
Sherlock Holmes, Consulting Detective: The Unauthorized Strategy Guide
Sid Meier's Colonization: The Official Strategy Guide
SimCity 2000: Power, Politics, and Planning
SimEarth: The Official Strategy Guide
SimFarm Almanac: The Official Guide to SimFarm
SimLife: The Official Strategy Guide
SSN-21 Seawolf: The Official Strategy Guide
Strike Commander: The Official Strategy Guide and Flight School
Stunt Island: The Official Strategy Guide
SubWar 2050: The Official Strategy Guide
TIE Fighter: The Official Strategy Guide
Ultima: The Avatar Adventures
Ultima VII and Underworld: More Avatar Adventures
Under a Killing Moon: The Official Strategy Guide
Wing Commander I and II: The Ultimate Strategy Guide
X-COM UFO Defense: The Official Strategy Guide
X-Wing: The Official Strategy Guide

How to Order:

For information on quantity discounts contact the publisher: Prima Publishing, P.O. Box 1260BK, Rocklin, CA 95677-1260; (916) 632-4400. On your letterhead include information concerning the intended use of the books and the number of books you wish to purchase. For individual orders, turn to the back of the book for more information.

Dragon Lore™
The Official Strategy Guide

Rusel DeMaria
and
Alex Uttermann

P

Prima Publishing
P.O. Box 1260BK
Rocklin, CA 95677-1260

Secrets of the Games is an imprint of Prima Publishing, Rocklin, California 95677.

Publisher, Entertainment: Roger Stewart
Managing Editor: Paula Munier Lee
Sr. Acquisitions Editor: Hartley Lesser
Creative Director, Secrets of the Games: Rusel DeMaria
Project Editor: Brett Skogen
Cover Production Coordinator: Anne Flemke
Copy Editor: Sam Mills
Technical Reviewer: Manny Granillo
Book Design and Layout: Rusel DeMaria
Cover Design Adaptation: The Dunlavey Studio
Special Image Processing: Ocean Quigley

Important:

ISBN: 1-55958-672-9
Library of Congress Catalog Card Number: 94-68404
Printed in the United States of America
95 96 97 98 CWO 10 9 8 7 6 5 4 3 2 1

Contents

Foreword

In the old days, the interface was the game. Sure, you added some bouncing pixels to the screen, but in so many ways a clever interface was the key to creating a fun and engaging contest on the digital screen. Not so, today. Recently, graphics have become the headliners, interface has become secondary, and game play has been squeezed in around the fantastic graphics.

Thank digital 3D technology and digital video for knocking the game industry on its ear. We're inventing new ways to tell stories and involve players. The trick is to combine, as seamlessly as possible, the graphics with the game elements.

That's what we've done in *Dragon Lore*. In this detailed world of fantasy, you'll be acting as young Werner von Wallenrod. As Werner, you interact with a variety of characters, fight if you must (or if you wish), explore, experiment, ponder, and ultimately take your chances at the Seats of Judgment.

We hope you enjoy this game, and because we have made some parts of it extra challenging, we also hope you enjoy this strategy guide. In it, Rusel DeMaria and Alex Uttermann have brought Werner's story to life while taking you (and Werner) along the wisest path toward becoming a Dragon Knight. By writing the game walkthrough as a fictional account, they've given you an added opportunity to lose yourself in the world of *Dragon Lore*.

DeMaria and Uttermann have also provided a more direct look at the game in the second part of this book. Between the two walkthrough sections, you'll find several pages of maps to help you navigate through the castle and the labyrinth.

This guide is your ultimate companion in the world of *Dragon Lore*. Keep it close by while you wander through this amazing digital landscape and attempt to solve its mysteries. And most of all, have fun! Explore! Enjoy!

Manny Granillo
Senior Producer
Mindscape, Inc.
Novato, CA
1995

In acknowledgment . . .

Retelling such a quirky tale as *Dragon Lore* has been a journey worth infinitely more than its own reward. There are so many people whose steadfast support contributed enormously to this process, but my thanks go first and foremost to my partner, Rusel DeMaria, who knows how to spot potential and give it room to grow. Seeing is believing. It's an honor and a privilege to know and work with you, querido.

Werner's search for a father he'll never know is a powerful theme to me. I've become fancifully convinced that the choice of Axel, that honorable father's first name (also an anagram of my own), was more than just a happy coincidence. It reminds me to acknowledge gratefully my own spiritual "fathers" — Jack Milak, Luis Garcia-Renart, Robert Kelly, Lee Hambro, Morrie Brenner, Boualem Bousseloub, Bart Snyder, Don Ehrman, John Bradshaw, Ludwig von Beethoven, Abuna Chacour, Robert Heinlein, Gil Scott-Heron, Henry Miller, Erté, Peter Gabriel, J.R.R. Tolkein and the Burning Man — invaluable teachers, all.

Further thanks to all the gamers in my life, Ibish and Gregor in particular, and Hules Bors, for showing me worlds within worlds and the importance of a lively story. Thanks to Alison Matulich for teaching the value of difficult choices and beautiful smiles. Also to Irma Buchheit, Katherine Moody, Teri Liston and Jeanne Starke-Iochman, for their constant reminders that life is one long adventure meant to be enjoyed, and to my soul brothers Howard Richman, Steve Wolf, and the other Alex, who loved me before I did.

Anne, Will, Carrol, Amy and John — glad you're all here. Mama and Papa, wherever you are — glad you've made it there. Andrea and Hank Courtois, kindred spirits, you're always in my heart. Someday we'll laugh about it all together. To my Al-Anon family, my love and gratitude, every day at a time. I couldn't have come this far without you all.

Final thanks go to the team at Prima Publishing, and Manny Granillo at Mindscape, for all the support. Les plus grands mercis à Cryo, for creating such a magnificent-looking game as *Dragon Lore.*

See you all from the mists, which lie just beyond that curve in the road!

Alex Uttermann

My thanks are simple. To my family, both new and old. To Manny, Cryo, and the growing multitude of Primates. To Querida, who really did it!

RDM

Introduction
What's in this Book?

Welcome to *Dragon Lore: The Official Strategy Guide*. We hope you will find this book useful while you're exploring Werner's world. We've tried to provide you with all the information you'll need to become a Dragon Knight and ride proudly on your very own von Wallenrod dragon.

To start you off, we've written a fictional treatment of the game, with Werner making the wisest choices he can. Following this "fictional walkthrough" is sure to get you elected. Reading this section from start to finish should give you a feeling of living the story with young Werner, and learning about this strange and beautiful world through his eyes and experience.

In the middle section of the book are all the maps for the castle, plus the labyrinth (where you encounter Kuru and Klaus von Straupzigo.

The third section of the book is a more concise walkthrough of the game, with information about which objects are to be found in each area. Because we've labeled each section of this walkthrough, you can use it as a reference and only look for information if you get stuck. We recommend using this section first if you don't want to know all the answers immediately.

Finally, we've offered some suggestions for other ways to play the game, plus some general guidelines.

We hope you're having a great time playing *Dragon Lore*. If our book can help you out, we're pleased. Whether your actions propel you toward force or wisdom, remember; it's not winning or losing that really counts. It's kicking Diakonov's butt out on a rail!

Fictional Walkthrough

PART ONE: TRAVELS AND TRIBULATIONS

My adventures began as many great adventures begin —
inadvertently.

It was a fine spring morning on the farm, as I remember, following a particularly difficult winter, in the 359th year of our Lord Harssk. This was the spring of my eighteenth birthday, and although I still felt like a boy, the course of events to follow would convincingly demonstrate otherwise. Though I must admit, I wasn't at all concerned with my future as a man on that fine day. I was much more interested in avoiding my chores.

We lived in a small farmhouse, my father and I, although we had several sizable pastures surrounding the main house. My father, a gruff and simple man, was constantly reminding me how important it was to care for the lands we owned, because they were so valuable in their own right. We farmed enough to feed ourselves and our cow and to have a bit left over to trade in the markets occasionally.

It was apparent to me that I wasn't cut out to be a farmer. I honestly couldn't see the sense in performing the same actions over and over again, year in and year out — the plowing, the planting, the harvesting, the milking of Daisy. There was no variation and no excitement in it, none at all. Yet it was all I knew, as I had been farming since my birth, or so it seemed. I often gazed longingly down the road, wondering what lay beyond Brutus, our snarling dog. The road forked outside our gates, and although the path to the right led to our various fields and pastures, the road to the left, once it passed the pond, our vegetable patch and Brutus, curved off to distant lands and many adventures. I was certain of it.

Although a bit of the chill still remained in the air, I was comfortable enough in my thin clothes. I always broke a sweat chopping wood, no matter the season. It was awfully difficult work. At least some joy was offered by the birds' singing, and I was more than a little distracted as I

came through the main gate, carrying my stack of wood for the woodpile. It was my habit to daydream about wielding a weapon of great power, like the wandering knight who had passed along our roads when I was but a young boy. I seized a tree branch that was on the ground in the yard, whirling around with it to ward off some unseen but probably dishonorable enemy. "Take that!" I

shouted, as I took a swipe at him. Of course, he was no more than a fly. I hit him, too, before I remembered my responsibilities to my father and tossed my sword, that is, my stick, a bit disdainfully, back into the corner of the yard.

My father was standing just outside the house, sharpening his knives, as always. A man of few words and much labor, I could tell how impatient he was with me this morning. Even though I'd already

done a score of tasks since I'd awakened at dawn, including chopping that infernal wood, he still wasn't satisfied. But then he hardly ever was, with me. As it turned out, that stupid milk pail was leaking again, so I'd have to go in search of some other vessel to replace it with temporarily.

The milking pail's leaking. See if you can find a bowl or something, Werner. Old Daisy has to be milked!

Daisy needed milking and couldn't be denied that all-important morning ritual. *Great,* I thought. *The course of my life is dictated by the needs of a cow. How fitting.*

The Search for the Bowl

I remembered that we had an extra bowl in the barn behind Schatzie, our other fierce dog who couldn't stand my scent. At least, I guessed that's what it was. Schatzie and Brutus were brother and sister, and they'd both hated me since I could remember. Of course, my chasing Schatzie around while pulling her tail or trying to ride Brutus like a horse when I was but a mere stripling probably didn't contribute to their overall fondness for me. My father swore that dogs were a man's best friend, but I thought I'd settle for a sword instead, any day. I just didn't get along with dogs too well. And I really wasn't about to march right into that field with the snarling, panting Schatzie, to take that bowl from

the barn without some kind of bribe for her. Not unless I wanted to return with my trousers shredded, or worse.

After some searching, I set off toward the smaller pasture, off to the end of the road to the right. There was usually a bone or even two to be found there, as the foolish dog would leave part of her

dinner behind in the shed, in her greedy enthusiasm to return to the pasture she so jealously guarded. And sure enough, a bone was more or less where I'd expected to find one, on the ground in the shed! I picked it up, and holding it out in front of me as I walked so that Schatzie would

smell the bone first (and not me!), I returned to the field where she guarded the fence. Some guard dog! The moment I gave her the bone, the simple-minded creature retreated docilely to her spot near the barn to chew it, wagging her tail all the way. With Schatzie thus occupied, I was able to walk right past her — though I confess I did keep a watch on her, from the corner of my eye — and pick up the bowl.

Triumphant that I had hit upon such a neat solution to this question of the leaking pail, and sure to win my father's praise for such cleverness, I turned back to the house whistling a merry tune, and gave him the bowl. There was certainly no praise, faint or otherwise, to be had from

him. All he had to say was that I needed to go fetch Daisy from the vegetable garden and tie her up in the other pasture so that he could milk her. So I followed him none too meekly into our simple stone house to get the rope from the wall. Couldn't tie the cow to a tree without it, after all. The last time I'd forgotten the rope, she'd managed to find her way back into the vegetables before I had time enough to blink. Of course, this had occurred the year before, and I hoped I was much wiser than that, now.

I went back outside again, and this time took the left fork, toward the vegetable patch. The green, lush mountains that I had admired this morning passed by in a blur, as their charms were lost on me in my

current state of resentment. *Fetch this, fetch that, Werner. Go get the cow who's in the garden — again.* I knew it was my fault that she'd gotten in there, but I really didn't care. I only hoped she hadn't broken the gate, again. It was rapidly becoming one of those days when I would have gladly forsaken farming forever, and continued off

down the mysterious road that curves to the left . . . but that was not to be. Nothing to be done except to follow my father's bidding and go get Daisy out of the vegetables, before she managed to eat all of the results of our recent planting.

As I entered the broken gate, all I could think was, *Great. He'll want me to fix this stupid gate, once I've got Daisy back into the pasture.*

Cursing all cows in general and this one in particular, I looked around for the mooing creature, and sure enough, there she was near the pond, chewing her silly cud. Well, at least some of the vegetables were spared. Content to have me throw the rope around her, and content to be led all the way back past Schatzie and into the far pasture, Daisy didn't seem to care that I was taking her away from Paradise, in the form of our vegetable garden. Once she was in the pasture, I merely followed her to her favorite milking spot near a tree, and tied her to it. This time, I made sure to tie good strong knots, for I wasn't keen on repeating this process—at least, not any time soon.

With Daisy securely tied in the pasture, I didn't have too much to do, other than to return to the farmhouse and let my father know that this task was accomplished. I entered our modest home in a state of trepidation, certain that his anger about my neglect of Daisy, coupled with news of the broken gate, would have reached a boiling point by now.

My Birthday "Party"

Whatever my expectations may have been, I couldn't have been more flabbergasted by the words of my father. "There's something I've got to tell you, Werner. I never told you before, because I had to wait 'til your eighteenth birthday. Well, that's today. So listen carefully now . . ."

Rendered speechless by his revelations, I listened to this simple farmer explain to me that I was not his son, after all. He gave me a mysterious, intricately carved ring, telling me that it was mine by right.

By right? He gave me a whistle, too, which I presumed was meant for Brutus' furry ears. Finally, he gave me his permission to take whatever I needed from the house, for I should need some things along my travels. The most he would tell me of the path ahead of me was, "My advice to you is to head to the Castle von Wallenrod."

An overwhelming sadness passed over me, as it dawned on me that all I had taken for granted, the security of our simple lives here on the farm, the daily routines, was no longer for me. I was to leave this place, to go in search of my true destiny. At this point, I was torn between a sudden sense of responsibility — if I left, who would take care of the farm, and the farmer? — and a fledgling sense of incredible freedom. The adventures I'd always dreamt of would happen at last, my origins were not as humble as I'd believed, and great quests would be won by my hand . . . I was free!

Stumbling over myself in my awkward haste to be free of this dirty, smelly stone house, I managed to get the shield off the wall, from its honorable watch over the stone fireplace. I'd always admired it, and had assumed that my father kept it as a family tradition of some sort. There was a lot I hadn't cared to know, and I certainly wasn't about to start prying now. I pulled down the suit of leather armor from the stand in the corner, and put it on immediately, my heart soaring with pride as I considered myself a well-armored knight, on a quest. Oh, I was so young then, and had no clearly defined idea of what adventure meant, other than a break from the monotony of life on the farm.

Anxious to be on my way, I nearly missed the yellow pouch of sulfur on the table, and the flint on top of the barrel. I pocketed them both, however, and took the canteen from the bed near my father — I mean, my adopted father. If he wasn't my father, then who was? On the way out the door for the last time, I turned again to ask for advice, or a blessing, or I don't exactly know what, from the farmer. I was eager to know where this castle with the peculiar name was, and why it had any importance to me at all. And why had the farmer sworn not to tell me anything more than this? And to whom had he sworn this? Oh, my mind was positively teeming with questions. The farmer must have sensed all of my queries and doubts, and perhaps more that I couldn't guess at, but he said only, "I'm sorry, Werner. From now on, you're on your own." And with that, he went back to sharpening his knives.

Getting the pouch of sulfur.

Farewell to the Farm

As I left the stone house I'd known for the past eighteen years, I was gripped with an intense momentary fear that I would never see it again. I decided to take one last turn around the house, etching it permanently in my memory. As I walked behind the house, a weapon lying in the grass caught my attention, a hammer that had

been here for who knows how long. I decided to take it along. After all, I wasn't sure that all of my travels were going to be peaceful ones! I came around to the front of the house to the old cart, where I found the curvy sword I'd played with, as a boy. Perhaps this wasn't really a

viable weapon, more a toy, really. It was a sword, though, and I imagined myself a great knight, wielding it.

I realized I was procrastinating a bit, dawdling around the yard looking for weapons when it was more than time to leave everything I'd known and go out seeking my fortunes. There was quite a lump

in my throat; I'm really not sure where it came from. Reminding myself that this was exactly what I'd desired for most of my eighteen years, the chance to go exploring the world without return to this misbegotten farm, I set off cheerfully down the curving road to the left, past the familiar pastures of my youth, for territories alien to me. When I reached Brutus, instead of giving the ugly pup the usual kick in the ribs, I blew the whistle the old farmer had whittled for me and had the satisfaction of watching Brutus step aside for me. The path lay ahead. It only needs my two feet upon it, I thought to myself, and translated thought to deed.

The Dolmens

As I walked amid the white stones, I came into an expansive area, larger than any place I'd ever seen, surrounded by a flat, misty plain and green, green grass. The mist was everywhere around me, lending an air of magic and mystery to this strange setting.

The path I was on was lined with enormous white stones, resembling obelisks. As I continued along, enchanted with this unfamiliar world, an enormous stone marked the intersection of this path with another. I walked around it, to the right. At the same time, I noticed the rise of a hill to my right, a hill which had two enormous human skull openings which led Harssk only knew where. I guessed they beckoned into caves of some sort. It turns out that I guessed right.

Quaking with curiosity, I went along the white-stoned path between the two leering skulls. This was adventure, surely! Before I reached the hillside, I turned to the left and veered off the path onto the grass. Without consciously choosing my course, I was going to enter the cave on the left. Cautiously ducking my head as I went in, I made my way into the first cavernous room. The damp stench of mustiness assailed me, and made my eyes water. I was seized by an embarrassing bout of sneezing which rendered me immobile for a few moments. The human skeleton lying on the ground didn't help my confidence much, either. I'd never seen such a thing before and I must admit to feeling a bit shaken for a moment by the sight of it. "Poor fellow," I muttered under my breath, wiping my nose. I profoundly hoped that I was not to be the next adventurer ending up like that.

As I explored the dank cavern, I spied a shining object on the ground, all the way in the rear of the place. Upon closer inspection, it

turned out to be a key of some sort. It certainly wasn't the skeleton's key, or if it had been once, it had long since ceased to be useful to the poor wretch. I decided that since it probably didn't belong to anyone at all, I'd better take the key along with me. So I picked it up. Further investigation of this dark, altogether unpleasant place failed to produce any other items of interest, so I decided to leave it at once and explore elsewhere.

My feelings were churning around as I exited the maw of the skull. On the one hand, I'd just had a famous adventure, exploring the inside of a cave and actually finding a mysterious key. On the other hand, I felt a bit disappointed. I'd found a key, sure, but what was the point of it? There was nothing to open with it. Besides, despite an ignoble sneezing fit, I hadn't encountered any serious threats to my person. As I crossed the grass over to the other skull, I was beginning to feel that I'd been a bit cheated on this fabulous adventure of mine.

Upon entering the second skull's mouth, this sentiment vanished entirely, never to return. I stood in front of an iron gate which was locked and wouldn't open. I was momentarily thwarted, but almost immediately put one mental image with another and produced the solution! The key I'd picked up was probably intended for this very gate. And so it was. As I used the key to open the gate, there was a kind of giddiness about me, a kind of arrogant pride in my good

fortune and excellent deductive reasoning. My pride, and much of my breath, disappeared as soon as I entered into this new cavern and heard an unearthly dry, rasping breathing. I was not alone!

Advancing toward me along the corridor to my right was a creature of vile form, an animated skeleton armed with a deadly halberd. My attempts to speak with this being, this raspy collection of bones, were useless. It seemed intent upon my destruction. Curbing the very natural instinct to run away, I armed myself as best I could with my hammer and prepared to defend myself against this monstrous creature.

I stepped into the hallway, just far enough so that I could take a few swipes at this thing while moving past it, down the hall. I certainly didn't want my back against the wall. This proved to be a good tactic, so I kept moving past the evil creature, turning to land a hit or two on it, then running past it again before it could manage to strike at me. The movement got to be very tiring after a few passes up and down the corridor, and the skeleton's stamina was intimidating. It was relentless. Just as I was feeling winded, and beginning to think that I could last no longer against it, I managed to sneak one final blow in and the skeleton crumbled with a shriek.

My relief at having preserved myself was the only thing in my mind. My senses were sharpened past possibility, my heart was beating a rapid tattoo in my chest. Leaning against the wall, I wiped the dust and sweat from my brow and steadied my breathing, which was uneven and panting, making me compare myself, uncomfortably enough, to Brutus and Schatzie.

As I looked down the corridor from whence the skeleton had come, I saw another gate and decided to go along until I reached it. When I came near the pile of bones which had been my enemy, I took the halberd it had been carrying before continuing my progress down the hall. I was midway through the corridor when, due to my heightened awareness of my surroundings, I noticed a small panel in the wall to my

right. As I went closer to examine it, I was sure it led to some mysterious clue about some mysterious . . . well, something, anyway . . . and I touched it, only to receive the second in a series of rather nasty scares. All I know is that a huge boulder came rolling out of nowhere, straight down the hall toward me. Fortunately, I leapt into an alcove behind me, acting purely on instinct, and the boulder continued thundering along its course down to the end of the corridor, where it crashed into pieces.

As the boulder came crashing toward me, some metal object in the rock flashed at me. It all happened so quickly, that I didn't have time

enough to react to it. The moment it was clear that I was safe, I recalled that shiny thing, and went to the site of the smashed boulder, kicking the fragments around a bit. Uncertain as to what I was looking for, I happened upon another key, much like the first one I'd come across, in the other skull. The first key had opened the gate which led me into this set of caverns. There

was another gate at the other end of the hallway, and it suddenly seemed pretty likely that this key would open that gate. I was on my feet before this thought even had time to fully mature, running to the end of the hallway to try this new key on the gate there. As it swung open, I shuddered to think what new ghoul awaited me beyond it. I fingered my hammer nervously, but there was no sinister presence to greet me at all, just a trap door in the floor.

"Well, Werner, you're certainly getting more than your share of excitement, today," I told myself, and, with some effort, lifted up the heavy door. It was a lot heavier than any pile of firewood I'd ever

carried, but I couldn't have cared less. Lifting it was much more exciting than lifting firewood. When it opened onto a basement room, I didn't think twice, just jumped right down. I wanted to see everything I could. As I'd happened into a torchlit chamber, which smelled a lot more pleasant than the last few places had, I was certainly not disappointed. Gone was that musty odor. This room, stately as it was, just smelled old. Really old.

There were two huge wooden doors down the stairs, with iron embellishments and what appeared to be a lock. These doors wouldn't open, and I'd run out of special keys. Stumped, I looked around the dimly lit room for answers, but there were none. I took the weapons I

had, and tried to beat the doors open with them, but to no avail. Finally, convinced that I must have something among my resources which would open this door, I looked through everything I owned. The flint and the sulfur were common items, my shield and weapons were of no use. I remembered the farmer telling me to take this, for I would need it — and stumbled across the ring! Taking the strange ring off of my finger, I held it up to the door. As it opened, I took a deep breath, in an attempt to prepare myself for whatever lay beyond. As usual, the sight which met my eyes wasn't one which I could ever have anticipated.

I tried to calculate how high the ceiling was in this domed room, based on the height of our stone house back on the farm, and was baffled. Three times the height? Four? I couldn't tell for sure. The floor itself was nearly the size of our biggest pasture, or so it seemed. There were torches everywhere along the walls, casting an eerie light about. But the vastness of this room wasn't by any means its strangest attribute. For one thing, there was an enormous wooden construction in the middle of the room, and for another, there was a green winged creature walking about on the shiny stone floors who was, I now know, a dragon! He, too, looked old. Really old. He also appeared to have been through many battles, as his claws were torn and his skin was scarred, here and there. Amazingly enough, his every step resonated off of the stone walls and sounded like thunder.

Based on the visible skeletons imbedded in the walls, my assumption was that this elaborately decorated box in the middle of the room must be a casket. Curious as to its contents, I timidly touched the end of it,

right through the chair back which blocked my view of it, somewhat. I had just time enough to glimpse a spectacular gem on the side of the lid. I was still holding the special ring, and my guess was that the ring had some significance, here. The dragon spoke to me the moment I touched the casket with the ring in my hand.

My prior experience with creatures having previously extended only to the likes of Brutus and Schatzie, I was genuinely startled that a creature like this could speak at all. That his voice should be so melodious and regal at the same time was also a shock. Obviously, this was a noble beast.

"By what right do you trouble the sleep of this Dragon Knight?" the dragon inquired. Speechless, I could only hold the ring, which was still in my grasp, out in front of me. The dragon noticed this ring, and had evidently noticed my glance at the ruby on the casket, as well, for he intoned, "Only one man may touch that ruby; he who places its twin beside it on the tomb!"

I thought about this for a long moment, as he continued, "The ruby's twin is in the Castle von Wallenrod." There was that name again! The Castle von Wallenrod. I had to get there. I just had to.

"The Dragon Ring you wear is not unknown to me. If you have the right to wear it, you should harness its power! That ring will channel the magic power that flows in your veins, but only if it is yours by right, and only if you bring it to life." And with this, he handed me a scroll. I was too unnerved by this whole exchange to examine it closely.

Before I had a chance to ask about where I might find the castle, or the implications of carrying a magic Dragon Ring, or any of this, the green dragon finished his remarks by saying something about how the

ring could be awakened if its owner and it were forged together by fire. I missed some of the details of this part, because I was so intent on my questions. But once he'd said this piece, he wouldn't respond to my questions at all. Nothing I tried would even get him to notice me after this point.

I pondered the dragon's comments as I left the room, and crawled up through the trap door again. A dragon had spoken to me. What did this mean, a Dragon Knight? Was that who was buried in this casket? I carried a Dragon Ring. A dragon had spoken to me. My adopted father had told me the ring was mine by right, so presumably I was its true owner. Did this mean that I had magic in my blood? I wasn't

exactly surprised by this possibility, but I was excited. I found my hands trembling as I opened the gate again to pass out of these caverns of death. A dragon had spoken to me!

As I stood outside the skull entrance once more, I realized that I still held the scroll that the dragon had given me. I eagerly unrolled it and looked at it now, but it was only a piece of parchment with the words Open Door scrawled across it. Disappointed, I tucked it away for future reference.

Dreamily wandering about, my head full of dragons and magic rings, I decided to take the path between the two skulls, up the hill. It was a steep climb, and as I reached the top I was stunned once more. This was a place of some import! Circled around the hilltop was a collection of stone chairs, huge ones, each with an insignia carved into the back of it. Behind the chairs were enormous pointed stones, one behind each chair, and in front of some of the chairs were — figures of people! There were some women, and some men, and most of them were armed, as well as peculiar-looking. Some of them were blue! All of them were frozen in position, like statues. I could walk around each of them, examine them, even try to talk to them, but they were not living. A little shaken, I had no idea what any of it meant, and as there was no one here who could explain this to me, I quickly went back down the hillside to resume my travels.

As I went back to the path which had brought me to the skulls, I came again across the enormous white stone in the center of the two paths' intersection. Again I went around it to the right, and came across a longer path lined with those perplexing white stones. As I went along the path, I saw that it turned to the right, under a series of archways constructed out of the same gleaming white stone. It was beginning to get chilly, and it seemed to me that the mist was closing in on me, when I caught sight of an exquisitely dressed man wearing a foreign sword on his back.

Chen Lai

I immediately disarmed myself, and went to speak to him. I perceived at once that his features were striking; he had hair darker than anyone I had ever encountered in my life, and eyes that were at once gentle and piercing. To my timid greeting, he responded cordially, and introduced himself as Chen Lai, Dragon Knight. So this was a Dragon Knight! At last I would discover what they were all about. Chen Lai must have seen my bewilderment, but I believe that he found something trustworthy about me, as well. This was a new experience.

In answer to my inquisitive expression, he responded in his odd accent, "Twelve Knights will vote, and you will become a Dragon Knight only if at least one half of our number decide in your favour!" I was having a difficult time understanding that I'd heard this correctly. I? Was to become a Dragon Knight? Was this true? And yet, a voice

I am Chen Lai... Dragon Knight. Twelve Knights will vote, and you will become a Dragon Knight only if at least half our number decide in your favour!

Will you choose the path of Power or that of Wisdom? Of Force or Mercy? Or will you take the narrow road that divides the two?

within me responded with so much acknowledgment and familiarity to this idea, that I was astounded. It was as if a part of me knew me in ways that the rest of me didn't know at all.

Chen Lai went on to explain that I had been judged on my actions during this whole day so far. I silently wondered by whom, but didn't bother to ask. I needed to listen as intently as I could, and see if I could really understand this Dragon Knight process. According to Chen Lai, my actions were balanced between Wisdom and Force, and if I kept along a path of Wisdom, I would keep his vote. So far, my actions had tended to be fairly wise.

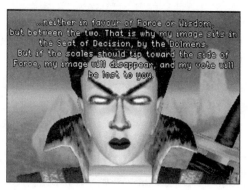

"That is why," elaborated Chen, "my image sits in the Seat of Decision by the Dolmens. But, if the balance changes, my image will disappear and my vote will be lost to you."

Just then, I recognized that this man in front of me looked just like one of the figures I'd seen up on the hillside. I was so struck by the honor and the obvious wisdom which emanated from the kindly eyes of Chen Lai that I vowed then and there to try to stay on the path of Wisdom. I had no taste for killing, I'd discovered, though I had done so without remorse when my own life was at stake. That is, if destroying a skeleton creature even constituted killing, in the first place. I also noticed that Chen was armed, and I was sure that he, too, was a worthy fighter if the situation warranted.

The Mountain Tunnel

I thanked Chen for his words, and we parted warmly. I went on along the path under the stone arches, through the mist, until it all parted and I was standing in front of some mountains which bore a marked resemblance to the mountains around my home at the farm. The air here was fresh, and clear, much like it had been back at home. A feeling of homesickness welled up in me, but a new feeling accompanied it. I was to be a Dragon Knight! I didn't have the time to waste thinking of farms, anymore. But the sound of an owl hooting close by was somehow comforting, nonetheless.

As I continued along the path, I came to a wooden door which had been built right into the mountain. As I pushed on it, it gave way with a terrific creak. I supposed that it hadn't been opened in a long, long time. Travelers probably hadn't been through here during the winter. The door opened into a tunnel, which made me tense at first, remembering the other experiences I'd had with underground places. There were no threatening skeletons here, however, so I walked right in and up to the next door. I figured it would open as soon as I pushed against it, but I was mistaken. It wouldn't budge. Confused, I tried many different ways to open the door, but none of my ideas were fruitful. Finally, I resigned myself to the idea that I might have to go

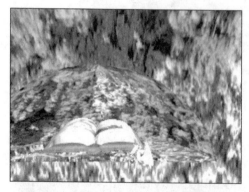

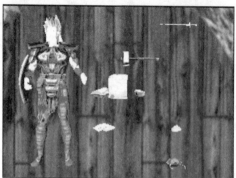

back out and find a different way around this mountain.

And that's when I saw it; the strange spot in the wall which looked like a hollowed-out alcove. As I tapped on it with my hammer, that piece of the wall crumbled and left behind a little shelf. The shelf had a book upon it, and as I picked it up and held it, turning it over and over again in my hands, I recognized that it was a book of spells. How did I know that? I just did. This was a Spell Book, and I was holding it! It was difficult to comprehend. Spells were magical, I knew that much. The dragon in the tomb had said that I had magic in my blood, which I at least hoped

was true. I think that's when I remembered the scroll, for recalling the dragon reminded me of it. I ripped out the parchment which said Open

Door on it, and put it into the book. It melted right in. *Open Door, aha. And I thought this door wouldn't open for me!*

Holding my breath, I looked carefully at the Open Door spell, and memorized the three magic symbols I saw there. I then looked at the door, and slowly recalled each symbol in turn, seeing them as clearly in my mind as though they were written there, instead of in a book. At last I gestured toward the door with my hand — and the door opened! Torn between babbling joy and total disbelief, I walked through the open door, pausing on the other side to collect my wits for a moment and put the Spell Book away before going any further.

At the Crossroads

I reached a point in this path where I had three choices of direction: left, right or straight ahead. The path ahead was blocked by an enormous spider web, and I wasn't too confident about encountering the creature

who had spun it. The path to the right appeared to lead to another cave. I figured I'd sworn off caves for a while, so I took the path to the left, and went into what appeared to be a house of some peculiar sort.

This house turned out to be a tavern, and the hosts were mighty peculiar, so at least part of my

observations were accurate. George and Albert stood behind the bar, and carried on a conversation which bored me, for the most part. Did they even care that I was there? The interesting part of it lay in watching them. George was a huge blue troll or some such creature, while Albert was some kind of dwarf. They were truly a fascinating pair. Albert rested on George's shoulders and cried out, "Not so fast! There's a little matter of a toll to be paid!" as I turned to escape their extremely dull observations about the weather and my stamina.

"That means money, heh, heh." George chuckled menacingly, at my back. I didn't like the tone in his voice, so I turned around to face him, again. Money?

This posed a grave problem for me, as I didn't have any money at all, so they determined that I'd have to earn my toll by performing a service for them. Albert explained, "You see, young fellow, George and I also earn a few crumbs making nectar

for dragons. You know what they are, don't you? Plenty of 'em round these parts." As I nodded my assent, he continued, "Now, to make the nectar, we take the resin from the hive of the

dragon fly. You passed it on your way here."

Since this didn't really sound so tricky to me, I agreed to collect some resin from the dragon fly's hive, for them to make their nectar. At George's prompting, "Don't forget the bit about the ladle, Albert," they gave me a ladle, and I went on my merry way.

The dragon fly hive turned out to be the cave down the path across from the tavern, so I went there to see the dragon fly. As I got closer to the hive, the bizarre scent of it got stronger and stronger, and I began to have second thoughts about this. Once inside, its lair smelled of a

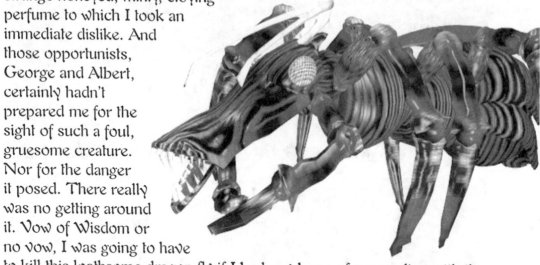

strange honeyed, minty, cloying perfume to which I took an immediate dislike. And those opportunists, George and Albert, certainly hadn't prepared me for the sight of such a foul, gruesome creature. Nor for the danger it posed. There really was no getting around it. Vow of Wisdom or no vow, I was going to have to kill this loathsome dragon fly if I had any hope of succeeding with the resin. I put the ladle away and pulled out my hammer.

The dragon fly proved to be a valiant enemy, but once I'd felled it, I was on the search for a full resin pot. Finally, I found it in the alcove in the back of the cave. The pot was practically dripping with resin, so I dipped the ladle into the resin, mindful of the warnings not to touch the gooey, nasty substance itself.

Now I had to carry this burden back to the inn, and relinquish it into the hands of mine hosts. Well, they were awfully happy to receive the resin. That is, once George remembered that he'd already met me. Albert was in raptures over the dripping ladle — "Full of resin, I see! Good work, young fellow." I tried not to think about the dead

dragon fly, or to wonder how disappointed they were going to be the next time they tried to get some resin. I also tried to remember my vow to act wisely, which spared George and Albert from my instinct to teach them a violent lesson about misleading innocent travelers about the inherent dangers of collecting dragonfly resin.

However, in the end, George and Albert turned out to be fairly decent fellows. They felt guilty for having misled me about the difficulties of resin retrieval, and so presented me, very kindly, with a few gifts. Never mind that these items had belonged to some other traveler — I certainly didn't let it bother me. The gifts included a wonderful weapon, a Morning Star. It seemed to be much more powerful than my hammer, and I was truly grateful for such a powerful gift. George and Albert also handed me a scroll. I figured it was a spell, and held it in my hand to check it, once outside the tavern. I hoped it was an important one. The third gift, a length of rope, was a trifle less interesting than the other two, but I remembered my manners and thanked them civilly for all three. And then I turned around, and left the tavern.

It was only when I reached the spider web that I realized how very grateful I was to George and Albert, and I even forgave them for the dragon fly incident. The spell they'd given me was a Fireball spell. I promptly put it in my spell book, and cast it upon the spider web. I wasn't exactly sure what a fireball was or what it would do exactly. The results were overwhelming, as a huge ball of fire went straight into the web and burned it all up. Just like that. And I had a cleared path once more. Sniffing the faintly smoky scent in the air, I strolled right under the arches, trying to appear as casual as possible, for someone who'd just unleashed an enormous ball of fire from nowhere.

The Ferry

My nonchalance didn't last very long, though. I came upon an intricately wrought structure, which I didn't think had been created by human hands. It appeared to be a gatehouse of some sort, as it was on a river with what seemed to be a ferry behind it. The moment I got close enough to it to hear the water running in the river, my stomach fell, and something told me that this was wrong, terribly wrong. I cautiously walked near the ferry, but could find no means to make it move, so I turned to go back into the gatehouse and was suddenly confronted by a dark, human-like figure from whom evil radiated so strongly that I could nearly touch it in the air around me. I could certainly feel it in my bones.

My instinct was immediate. Taking up the Morning Star, in a frenzied desire to rid this land of such a malevolent being, I aimed

carefully at his head and struck. Or, at least, I thought I did. It seemed to me that somehow my blow was deflected, or frozen in mid-air, or simply hit the air where this black-clad figure of doom had been standing, not a moment before. However it happened, I could not now strike against him.

Amid his jeering laughter, he chided me, "Can't find the barge-pole, eh? Well, farm boy, if you want to reach the castle, you'll have to keep your eyes open!" Frightened that this awful creature knew me, while I didn't know him, I remained mute. The sudden, wild suspicion that he could be a Dragon Knight crossed my mind, only to be banished — Dragon Knights were honorable, were they not?

But my questions were not to be answered at this time. With his grating laughter still echoing through the small building, he vanished

and left in his wake a hideous green monster wielding an enormous cleaver. It must have outweighed me at least three times over. Like his master, this creature, too, seemed set on my destruction. I swung my mace as accurately as I could, for a newly initiated fighter with such a new weapon in his hands. For a split second I was aware of a wave of fear crashing over me — what if this monster proved stronger than I was? — but my rage at being left to fight a mere minion by a cowardly villain overpowered any fears I had. I kept moving to keep out of range of that deadly cleaver, using the superior reach of my morning star to strike the beast before it could strike back. Discretion was definitely the better part of valor in this case, and I was able to vanquish the creature without taking so much as a scratch from its blade.

As the monster died, he emitted a sound that was so haunting and ghastly that it froze my blood, and a scent of mindless evil that I still remember to this day. Not relishing the process overmuch, I searched the collapsed creature's carcass as quickly as I could. I was frightened that his master would

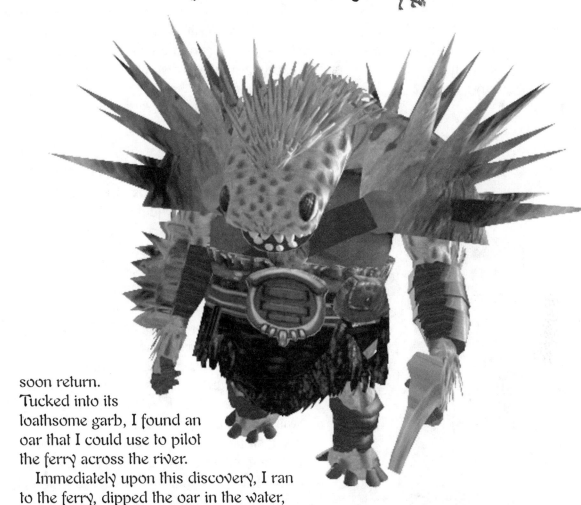

soon return.
Tucked into its
loathsome garb, I found an
oar that I could use to pilot
the ferry across the river.

Immediately upon this discovery, I ran
to the ferry, dipped the oar in the water,
and so paddled across the river until I reached the other side safely.
Truly, I was looking back over my shoulder the entire way, hoping

against hope that the black fiend would not reappear to cause me harm. Still panting a bit from the exertion and the sentiments of fear which drove me forward, I reached the other side and disembarked from the barge at once.

Formar Thain

The moment my feet hit the ground, I was unaccountably comforted. Somehow, the feel of good, hard ground beneath my feet was the magic remedy to my fears. Cheered by this development, I took a few steps, and put my mace away. There was a blue man with white hair walking not ten paces from me. I recognized him as the physical manifestation of one of the Dragon Knight figures from the Seat of Decision in the Dolmens. Without a shadow of a doubt, I knew that this man meant me no harm, and that I could trust him. He was pacing around underneath a series of great stone arches, which caused a kind of tunnel effect above us, as I joined him. Up close, I noted that the blueness of his skin, though strange to me, was one of the most beautiful things I'd ever seen along my travels. The shock of white hair only served to emphasize the contrast between his youthful countenance and his sage-like smile. His ears were pointed, and his eyes, which looked very old indeed, were kind and wise. They twinkled a bit as he considered me for a moment, before introducing himself.

"I am Formar Thain of Hav'shal. We shall meet again when the voting begins." I trusted this kindly Formar instantly.

"You have come far, Werner von Wallenrod. You have your father's courage." As he said this, I felt a chill go through me. I would probably never get used to meeting people who already knew me by name, though I was coming to some terms with this prospect. But meeting someone who knew my father was downright eerie. Why, I hadn't even known my own sire!

Although I was beginning to have a good amount of confidence in my talents as a fighter, having left several casualties in my wake, I did not need Formar's urging to remain upon a path of Wisdom. Mostly, I appreciated the comparison of me to my father, more particularly to my father's wisdom. I had been given my first gift — although I knew nothing of my father, I now knew him to be a wise man! Perhaps my father would be proud of me. Where, then, was he? Did he await me in the Castle von Wallenrod? I, too, would be so wise as he, I hoped.

My only reservation was that my actions might not have been judged according to the situations which prompted them. It concerned me that my acts of violence would be considered foolish — else why the warning? — and yet, in the cases of the walking skeleton, the dragon fly, and the green minion of that dark man, I had merely defended myself against very real threats to my own existence. I had trusted my instincts. Surely these actions could not be deemed anything but wise! I had no desire to kill without reason — nor did I find it reasonable that anyone or anything should want to kill me.

Tanathya's Garden

I continued along the pathway underneath the vast stone arches, until I reached a curious place. My surroundings had changed abruptly; I appeared to have entered a ruined garden of some sort.

Bits and pieces of pillars were scattered randomly about. The air was humid, and heavy with the scent of plants that were foreign to me. The flies were everywhere! I found myself slapping at my arms, my legs, trying to shoo them out of my face. Their incessant buzzing was annoying and so preoccupied was I with my futile attempts to rid myself of these obnoxious insects, that I only narrowly missed becoming a meal for the hideous, man-eating plant in the rear of the garden. Never in my life have I seen a plant so huge — it was taller than I was, and I was no stripling! I sensed immediately that it intended to capture me in its tentacles, so I stayed back from it and considered my options.

I had reached the end of this garden, and the plant was against a wall. It seemed more than likely that I would want to find myself on the other side of that wall, somehow. Yet I dared not come so close to the wall as to be within reach of that plant. As I was mulling it over, I noticed an oddly shaped skull to the right of the plant. It was the skull of some horned creature which clearly had provided a repast of some sort for the plant. I sighed deeply in recognition, and picked up the skull. A vague

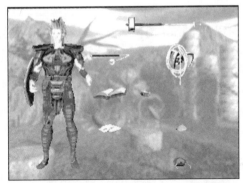

plan was forming in my mind. To the left of the plant was a tree whose branches looked strong enough to hold my weight, at least long enough for me to vault up to the wall. But how to scale it without arousing the interest of this floral freak of nature?

Once again, I had cause to thank George and Albert silently. They had given me a good length of rope, which, when tied to the horned skull, would provide me with a fair chance to get over the wall. All I had to do was make sure I managed to hook the skull firmly on the tree branch. My first throw held, and I went up and over the terrible plant and the inviting wall in a pretty smooth motion. Something in the pit of my stomach told me there were no second chances.

Tanathya

I landed on the other side with little grace, and a huge thud. This was a bit embarrassing, as there was a comely young woman watching me from behind a tree, a sardonic little half-smile forming on her lips. Truthfully, I had never seen such a beautiful girl in my life! I felt like a churl for scrutinizing her so closely, but I  couldn't help myself. She was dressed in a sparse, war-like garment which fascinated me, and the light in her eyes bespoke a glittering

challenge to me. I went to stand up, and realized I still had my makeshift grappling hook in my hand, so I quickly stowed it away among my possessions. Awkwardly, I brushed myself off as best as I could, and went toward her. I tried to think of an intelligent greeting, for I very much wanted this woman to like me.

"So you got past my wall!" she replied to my stammered salutation, almost disdainfully. Was she disappointed that I had? It suddenly occurred to me that most people didn't, and I gulped to consider my narrowly missed fate as some maniacal flora's lunch.

Ignoring my discomfiture, the woman continued, "I am Tanathya, Dragon Knight." I hoped that I didn't look too surprised by this disclosure. I managed to disguise my involuntary choking sound as a cough. I don't think she noticed anything amiss, for she went on, "And you are wearing the Dragon Ring of the von Wallenrods. Who are you?" That's when she stared me down. Although I knew by now that I had a rightful claim to the ring I wore, I felt like an interloper, and guilty of some unspeakable crime.

I studied my boots for a moment, and then raised my head to return that impenetrable gaze of Tanathya's. I would not be made to feel foolish. I, too, would be a Dragon Knight someday. I spoke calmly, looking straight into her forbidding eyes. "I am Werner von Wallenrod, Lady Tanathya, en route to the Castle von Wallenrod. My claim is just, and my ring my own."

Her eyes flashed briefly, registering my words. She considered me for a long moment, before saying reprovingly, "Getting into the castle won't be easy, Werner. And even if you make it, you'll become a Knight only if at least half the Dragon Rings are for you!"

I shrugged impatiently. I'd already heard all about that from Chen, and I intended to win those votes. Tanathya wasn't finished with her lecture, though. "There are twelve Dragon Knights living. There's also Fujitomo: he's dead, but his Dragon Ring has not yet been claimed. If you get it, that will be a vote for you."

Was she trying to be helpful? Perhaps I would have her vote, as well! Her next words banished that piece of arrogance from me.

"As for my vote, you'll have to earn it!" And she looked me up and down, from head to toe, as if I were a piece of livestock at the county fair up for auction! "I like men whose souls are made of steel, and whose blades are red with blood!" she proclaimed.

Inwardly, I groaned. Just my luck, the only female Dragon Knight I met was the one who had more than a mere taste for blood. Under other circumstances, I would eagerly have done anything she asked of me. Yet I had sworn myself to a path of Wisdom. With difficulty, I summoned up the images of Chen Lai and Formar in my mind, and promised that I could not disappoint these two. Ah, but the approval of Tanathya! How could I leave her as my enemy?

She must have taken some kind of liking to me, though, because she had, after all, mentioned the ring of Fujitomo. This reflection cheered me a bit. Perhaps we wouldn't have to be enemies, after all.

Although I could have rested in this place many an hour, staring into the dark eyes of Tanathya, it was clear to me that not only was she impatient for me to be gone — but so was I! With difficulty, I took my leave of her and continued on my way, down the path behind her.

The Mushroom Village

Eventually the path brought me to a crude wooden bridge that crossed over a small stream. Ahead of me there was what seemed to be an entire village of toadstools, giant ones. Upon closer observation, it appeared that there were little homes carved in among these mushrooms. I wondered what kinds of creatures would inhabit such tiny abodes. Were they faeries, like the old tales spoke of? Fascinated, I wandered amid the little homes, without seeing any of those mythical beings. Finally, I came across a blue woman, whom I immediately recognized as a Dragon Knight.

She hailed me at once, and at once chided me. "A pity you're too big to visit the people in the toadstools! They welcome friendly visitors their own size!"

She, too, addressed my by name. It was evident that she knew exactly who I was and what I sought. "I am Chelhydra, and I wear a Dragon Ring. Prove yourself to be Wise and you will have my vote."

Her forceful, almost confrontational way of speaking seemed to me at odds with her gentle words and advice. I realized that Chelhydra, a wise Dragon Knight, was a complex individual. On the one hand, she was armed to the teeth and commanded a great deal of respect. She certainly had mine. On the other, she obviously had an enormous concern for the comings and goings of the little people in this village. And yet, I could have sworn that she was teasing me a bit about my height! Oh, Chelhydra was a contradictory creature, to be sure.

Like Formar, Chelhydra had the smooth, beautiful blue skin which spoke to me of distant lands and ancient wisdoms. I wondered about the dark blue star over her eye, which did not appear to be a part of her natural skin. Was this worn for ceremonial reasons? Had she gotten a kind of tattoo as a rite of passage among her own people? Although I wanted to ask, I restrained my impulsive curiosity and listened instead to what she had to say.

As to the animosity between Tanathya and Chelhydra, although I was curious about it, I knew enough to stay out of a conflict that was probably older than I was. I had my own demons to fight, without getting involved in the battles of others, though the words of Chelhydra rang strongly in my ears, "If she votes for you, you may be sure I vote against!"

She concluded by saying, "The sprites who live in those toadstools are friends of mine. If you do decide to pay them a visit, I'll be watching." And then she would say no more.

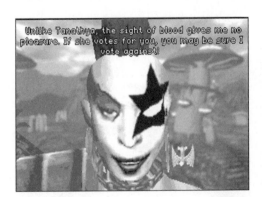

I figured, based in large part upon the obscure chiding of Chelhydra, that I'd want to find something to make me small enough to enter the mushroom village. I was delighted to think that I could actually have the chance to converse with sprites and faerie-folk. It also seemed pretty clear to me that whatever it was that I sought, I wasn't going to find it here, in the mushroom village. I walked around the outer side of the toadstools, along the creek, until I came to another wooden bridge, much like the one I'd come across before. I decided to cross it and see where it might take me.

The Fountain

I came into a deserted clearing which had a great fountain in the middle of it. It was colder here than it had been in the mushroom village, and much more desolate. Everything here was grey, and a bit dusty. Even the trees were bereft of leaves. The only pleasant aspect of the clearing was the cheerful sound of the water falling in the fountain. Fortunately,

it seemed that there were a number of paths to take from here, so that I wouldn't have to remain in this lonely little spot for very long.

The Dark Faerie

I walked around the path to the right, and decided to take the first path I came to. It was covered partially by a half-dead weeping willow tree, which I didn't take as such a positive omen. Pushing the scraping branches out of my way, I went down the path. As the path progresses, the icy winds came up and it got cold, and colder . . . and

colder, until I was shivering in my breeches. Finally, I stepped out onto an arctic plain, ringed by distant mountains. *The weather is certainly strange enough in these lands,* I thought to myself. *One minute it's warm and the air is heavy, and the next minute it's icy and overcast.*

As I looked around, I saw a bundle of apples on the ground. I realized how hungry I was, and promptly wolfed a few of them down. I had little concern just then for my surroundings, so I was actually surprised when I finally looked up from the apples and saw a treehouse looming above me. This aroused my deepest curiosity, so I went looking for a way to reach this house. There was no ladder, no stairs, nothing. Just a house situated way up in a tree. It had a door on it, so I concluded that there must be a way to access the entrance, as well. Otherwise, why have a door at all?

At this point, I heard the sounds of a growling beast, and looked to my right, from whence the sound emanated. There was a fierce-looking beast, grotesque beyond description, whose demeanor was so much like Brutus' that I nearly burst out laughing. Only, of course, this was no laughing matter. This furry monstrosity was quite clearly the guardian of the house, and I would somehow have to get by it to access the treehouse above. As I was pondering what action to take, I noticed that the creature was eyeing me and licking its lips. My initial reaction

to this was to have my mace handy.
Well, it was cold and I wasn't
necessarily thinking too clearly.
My second reaction was to
realize that I still had an apple
in my hand, and that this
poor animal was obviously
displaying all of its interest
in the apple, not in me.
Ah, the relief. I quickly
gave the apple to the
grateful beast, and it
moved aside, munching
happily. I had
encountered a plant
that ate flesh, but I had
not yet encountered
so fierce a
creature who
ate plants! As
it moved to my
right, I found the very
thing I'd been
searching for. There
was a lever in the ground,
and I guessed that pulling it would transport me to
the treehouse.

This proved to be correct. As I pulled upon the lever, a gust of that icy wind suddenly blew up even stronger, as if out of nowhere — or everywhere — and carried me, weightless and shivering, all the way up to the top of the tree.

Once in the treehouse, I was amazed at how dilapidated the woodwork was here. Didn't anyone really care for all of this? The whole house was open, and though it was cold, at least there was a relief from the winds. This was a great reprieve, as my hands were practically blue with cold and had long since ceased to have much feeling about them. Rubbing my hands together vigorously as I looked around the house, I saw a tree in the center of it. There was a cut-out area in the pillar, and behind it, an old gray-haired faerie. I could tell that this old woman was a faerie, because she had enormous silver and orange wings and she knew me by name. I refused to be prejudiced by the skull insignias on her thigh. Eager to speak with her, as I was sure she could give me something to make me small enough to enter the mushroom village, I encouraged her to talk to me.

But something was deadly wrong about this, I could feel it. "So, you gave my greedy little Puss an apple, did you?" she chided me in a voice which sounded like one metal knife blade rubbing against another. "That was much too kind . . . better beat him, you know. Much better to send him away to lick his wounds." I was truly shocked by this, but more shocked by her offer to give me great powers. For killing.

"Wouldn't you like that, Werner?" For a moment, I wondered if this old frightful faerie was in league with Tanathya, but I dismissed that

Take this key. It opens a door in a tunnel, not far from here. Go and grasp your destiny... It's not difficult, you'll see!

notion as a fanciful one. For one thing, Tanathya would have made mincemeat out of this old harpy in less than the wink of an eye.

Well, she gave me something, all right — a key to use in a tunnel, "not far from here." When I took it from her wrinkled hand, she grasped mine momentarily. Her cold claw scared me. "Go and grasp your destiny . . . it's not difficult, you'll see!" Not exactly what I was looking for, although I supposed that there would be a tunnel to explore somewhere along my travels. Perhaps this key would come in handy. Oh, well.

I pocketed the key and was overcome with the desire to leave this frigid place immediately. I walked out the door I had entered, and found another lever to my right. As I pulled it, that weird wind came up again — only it went backward, this time. I really couldn't have explained it too clearly, but I was airborne for a few moments and then I was back down on the ground again. After

one last compassionate glance at the poor Puss, who was still munching the apple, I headed back to the dark, craggy mountains, searching for the path out of this frozen wasteland.

The Sunlit Faerie

As I returned again to the fountain, it seemed bright and cheery by comparison to the tundra I'd just crossed to get here. The merry melody of the rushing water was music to my ears, and it was a whole lot warmer here than it had been in that land of ice and snow. Had I truly considered this clearing desolate, before? It seemed quite welcoming now. I rested for more than a moment at the fountain, until my hands had some sensation in them again, and my feet were quite thawed out. I looked across the way, and decided to take the path I saw there, which was also marked by a weeping willow. This tree wasn't nearly as dry as the one in front of the path to the white-haired faerie had been, nor was it obstructing the path.

As I walked along, it seemed to me that the air filled with light fragrances, as though all of the perfumes from the trees and flowers were parading through it, one by one. The weather was considerably

warmer, and as I turned a corner in the path, the sight of a beautiful, wooden, castle-like tree house met my wondering eyes. I had to cross a quaint wooden bridge to reach this house, and all around me the sounds and smells of spring were evident. Even the water rushing gaily under my feet, as I marched over the bridge, sang a bright song of birth and growth. I knew no reservations as I entered this house. Somehow I was sure that not only was I expected, but I was welcome, too.

As I entered the warm house, I climbed a shallow set of stairs and came up at the top of them, facing a ladder. This sight was somehow not in keeping with my experiences; other doors I had passed through opened up onto whole rooms, but this one opened to face a ladder. Surprising, at the least. As I looked up and down the hallway, I saw small but comfortable rooms, on either side. For a short time, it seemed that I was alone, and so at my leisure to admire the trappings of this cozy home. There were stone turrets and huge, high beams. This was a peaceful little fortress.

A rustling sound came from one of the other rooms, and as I turned to determine the cause of the sound, a blonde faerie of graceful proportions came toward me. Ordinarily, I would have felt out of place, entering the home of a stranger like this, and a magical faerie at that! But this was a warm and welcoming place, one in which I felt myself to be at home. The faerie's kindness and generosity only served to reinforce this sense of mine.

She did in fact expect to see me . . . "You're Werner, aren't you?" she asked, in her gentle tones. At my nod, she went on with a smile, "There is something I want you to do for me. Take this cog." I looked at the thing. It was unprepossessing and mercifully light enough to carry with no problem.

I took it. I must have looked a bit doubtful, for she reassured me, "You'll soon find something to put it in."

When I persisted in trying to determine where I would find a use for the cog, she gently responded, "Just put the cog back in its place," adding, "and don't listen to what my sister tells you." This sweet, maternal creature was related to that other vile winged biddy? As difficult as I found this to believe, I kept my disbelief to myself.

Once the faerie gently reprieved me for talking so much, I realized that I was given leave to go. She wanted to help me further, but simply didn't have the time to do so. Before leaving, I went upstairs to her bedroom,

searching for anything that would help me to become small enough to visit the sprites. The room was airy and light, and I stood still for a moment, swaying with the gentle sound of faerie bells.

In the small chest of drawers across from her bed, I found a piece of flowered cloth. As if from a dream, I understood that she had left the drawer open for me, and that I was meant to have this cloth. I picked it up, and went down the stairs and out the door without another word, as I prepared to return to the mushrooms to seek entry to the sprite village.

As I retraced my steps over the bridge and back to the fountain, the sunny scents of springtime got fainter and fainter, the more I walked. Finally, I found myself back at the fountain. My heart was heavy; I

missed the sunshine and the joyful spring sounds and scents which had surrounded the faerie woman's home. Thoughtfully, I took the piece of cloth and examined it. It didn't look too special, just like an ordinary square of material with a flowered print all over it. It carried with it the scent of the faerie woman's house and yard, though, and I inhaled the exquisite perfumes, breathing deeply as though the beauty of the scents would ward off any evil. Since I was feeling a bit warm, I dipped the cloth in the fountain, and put the wet cloth on my forehead.

The Garden

Then I proceeded along the only path around the fountain I had not yet taken, the first one I reached as I moved to the left. As I walked along the path, there was a lot of pollen or some such ticklish substance in the air. Its presence increased as I walked, so it seemed like a good idea to leave the wet cloth over my face, although I moved it down from my forehead until it covered my mouth and nose. Another bout of uncontrolled sneezing would have been too much for my ego to bear, just then. I was, after all, going to be a Dragon Knight. As I continued along the path, I stumbled upon the source of the irritating dust in the

air — a garden filled with exotic flowers and weeds in full bloom.

As enchanting a sight as it was, this garden didn't seem all that inviting to me. For one thing, those flowers put out so much pollen that I probably would have collapsed, had I not been wearing the hastily constructed mask of wet faerie cloth. Since this was the last place near the fountain to visit, I suspected that there was a connection of some sort between the flowers and the toadstool village (although why a bunch of tiny people would want to have any contact with such potentially lethal plants was beyond my comprehension). Gingerly, I

picked a bunch of the purplish flowers, and two small bunches of the yellow and white ones. Even through the mask, the scent and the irritants these plants emitted was enough to make me dizzy. As I went to touch the red ones, I saw that they were heavily thorned, and thought better of picking any of them. Anything so well-armed was probably that way for a reason, or so I'd learned on the farm. Best to leave well enough alone. The same philosophy applied to the path I noticed beyond the red flowers, at least for the time being.

The Mushroom Village Again

With the flowers in hand, I returned to the fountain. Intent upon meeting some sprites, I hurried back across the paths until I reached the one wending its way between two light brown rocks, and I was crossing the bridge over the little creek again in no time. The twinkling lights of the mushroom homes seemed friendly, welcoming and full of promise to me.

I saw the Lady Chelhydra once more, but I did not seek out her company this time, for exploring this village of toadstools seemed much more important to me.

Walking until I reached what looked like a large, prominent mushroom, I paused to consider the best course to follow. In my possession, there were three bunches of flowers. Sheepishly, I realized that I was still wearing the mask of flowered cloth, and I took it off, hoping none of the nearby sprites had noticed it wrapped around my jowls. My, but I did feel foolish. I decided to take a closer look at the flowers I held, and as I did so, without the mask on, the blue flower gave off such a delicious odor that I actually took a bite out of it!

Perhaps my readers will at this moment believe that I had taken leave of my senses; what occurred next was so fantastic as to sound preposterous. And yet, I found myself shrinking down, down, down

until the toadstools loomed above me and the grasses which I had walked through assumed forest-like proportions. Enchanted with this transformation, I was startled from my delight by the unmistakable sound of approaching danger. Instinctively, I reached for my Morning Star, and tried to find an escape route for myself. To be trapped by some awful creature, in a strange habitat, simply for lack of room to run, seemed to me a most undignified fate — and one to be avoided at all costs. As I was running toward the creek, I caught sight of the danger — a menacing red scorpion which was coming for me!

Assured that I was in a clearing that permitted me enough mobility, I allowed the scorpion to get close enough to me that I could hit it.

While swinging wildly with my mace, I remained watchful of its stinger.
I knew all too well what damage a regular scorpion could inflict upon a
human of normal size. The thought of the consequences to my new,
tiny person was not worth dwelling upon. Mostly I tried my best to
stay out of its way, hitting, then running, and hoping to inflict whatever
pain I could to the venomous beast, whenever it got within range. This
was by far the most tiring battle I'd ever faced, striking at and dodging
the potential blows of this scorpion. My footwork remained animated,
and as the sweat poured down my
face, it became increasingly
difficult to concentrate on the
creature's movements. Yet I
couldn't afford to take my eyes off
of it, not for a moment.

    After what seemed like an
eternity of running, striking, and
dodging, the deed was finished at
last and I laid the scorpion to rest.
Shaking my head at the simple
irony that I'd nearly lost my life to a creature I would normally consider
harmless, I sat down on the ground to compose myself before meeting
any pixies. "If she's so bloomin' wise," I muttered to myself, "at the least

Chelhydra could've warned me about the scorpion." Fatigued, sweating, and chilled by the sight of the fallen red carcass nearby, I rested for a moment and took stock of my surroundings. As I looked about the mushroom village, I spied a blue bottle on the ground. Intrigued, I went over to it and picked it up. It appeared to have a harmless liquid in it, which gave off a faint whiff of faerie springtime. The potion had a wonderful scent to it; I was thirsty and I drank it all, draining the bottle to the last drop. I waited for any profound changes to happen to my form, but was disappointed (although I did suddenly feel light-headed and refreshed, as if I'd just awakened from a full night's sleep).

Finally, I felt strong enough to go and investigate the mushroom houses. I walked about until I found the largest one in sight, and as I entered the toadstool was completely surprised to discover a finely constructed staircase. I hadn't been entirely certain about what to expect with sprites, since I'd heard so many different stories, and didn't know that they were capable of, or even interested in, building in the way that humans do. The stairs were shallow enough that I took them two at a time. It was difficult to realize that I was actually inside a mushroom, despite the warm, organic walls and the faintly fungal odor.

As I made it to the top of this rather winding staircase, I entered a room which was beautifully furnished in wooden furniture clearly carved by master sprites. A grateful sprite stood in front of me, and thanked me in an airy, sing-song voice for having rid his community of that wretched scorpion.

He gave me a scroll, which delighted me. I had a touch of sprite magic to take back with me to my world, and as this doesn't happen to one every day, such a special gift touched me greatly.

Then the sprite said, "I'd invite you into my home, but the effect of the flower you ate will soon wear off. Imagine what would happen if you grew to your normal height while you were inside a toadstool!"

I shuddered expressively.

"We have friends among your people," continued the sprite, "and we make a special potion for them." It seemed imperative that I find some of it, and without delay. I departed at once to find it.

As I left the house, I bore around to the left and near the creek, until I came across another such home, across from this one, in a very large toadstool. As I entered it, the sight of a stairway identical to the first led me to wonder whether I'd walked back into the sprite's home by mistake. It turned out to be a different home, which was clear as I entered the room at the top of the stairs. There were no sprites here, so I looked around the room until I saw a cabinet next to the bed,

containing a variety of tear-shaped bottles of a green liquid. So certain was I that this green stuff was in fact the potion to which the sprite had alluded, that I didn't stop to consider waiting for the owner of this place to return. Based on the words of the sprite, I suspected that I didn't have a lot of time to waste, and asking anyone's permission to use some of the potion seemed pointless. I just took one of the bottles, and beat a hasty retreat out of the toadstool home.

Once outside in the moist, fresh air, I gulped down the bottleful of green potion and waited for its effects. The transformation from my pixie size to my regular size wasn't nearly as much of a shock as the earlier, big-to-small transformation had been. I was a bit saddened that I could not stay

longer with the sprites, for I had appreciated the forthrightness and the kindness of the one sprite I did meet. Although I was set on a proud

course and would soon become a Dragon Knight, I had a fleeting desire to forget all about my destiny and stay among the sprites, drinking pixie brew and exchanging stories around their campfires. Like Chelhydra, who greeted me once again, I had quite a soft spot for the little people of the toadstools.

"You've shown courage and wisdom, Werner. When it is time for your election and you have on balance avoided needless violence, you may count on my ring." She smiled.

Glowing not only with the pride I felt at receiving the approval of the enigmatic Chelhydra, but also with the warm knowledge that I had

forged a common bond with her, I made my way back to the other bridge over the creek, the one which would take me through the fountain area once more. I felt in my heart a kinship with Chelhydra, more so than with any of the other Dragon Knights I had thus far encountered. We both had a

special feeling for the sprites. I envisioned a future in which I might share with Chelhydra the responsibility of watching over them, and it was a lovely vision.

Light in step and whistling a tune again, I was happy enough to be moving on from here. And so I crossed the bridge and returned to

the fountain. This time, I went straight ahead and to the left of the fountain, back to the path which led through the dark, craggy rocks. My intentions were to follow the path beyond the red flowers in the garden, to see where it would lead me.

The Stone Building and the Labyrinth

My first thoughts upon seeing the innocuous stone building ahead of me were of mild disappointment. I had come to expect strange and glorious sights around every bend in the road, and had almost forgotten that regular buildings with corresponding functions still existed. Perhaps I was a bit overindulged, in all of my newfound adventuring. On second look, though, the ornamental eaves served to remind me I was in a strange and exotic environment. Nothing was truly ordinary in this land.

The man pacing around in the courtyard, too, was anything but disappointing. He was garbed in bright stripes of red and black, bearing a strange pair of wings on his back. Even his helmet and boots reflected this winged motif! Ah, but he was a colorful sight in this otherwise dull place. Although I suspected him to be a Dragon Knight, due to his weathered face and noble bearing, it was still most satisfying to hear him say it, himself.

"Werner von Wallenrod, I am Kuru, one of the twelve living Dragon Knights." His curt manner spoke volumes about his impatience.

I soon discovered the reason for this. "My image," he stated brusquely, "does not sit in the Dolmen Seat! You are too weak, von Wallenrod. The balance swings the way of Mercy. There is no steel in your heart!"

So, I thought to myself, *Tanathya has friends. She is not the only one who urges me to violence.*

Werner von Hallenrod, I am Kuru, one of the 12 living Dragon Knights.

My image does not sit in the Dolmen Seat! You are too weak, von Hallenrod. The balance swings the way of Mercy. There is no steel in your heart!

Although I had a great deal of respect for this intense man, I had no desire to betray my true intentions to him. The path of honor and wisdom had become a shining goal for me, and I had no desire to deviate much from it. I wanted to prove myself brave and capable as a fighter, certainly, but there was no mindless killing in my conscience.

I knew that there was plenty enough steel in my heart, but that there was something else there as well. Honor was rapidly becoming an action to me, not just a vague word I'd heard along my travels. The truth was, as much as I wanted to win the respect and approval of the wiser Dragon Knights, there was an emerging part in me, a stronger voice which steered me toward honor and courage. That part of me wanted to act as wisely as I could and to conduct myself in an honorable way, so that I could have respect for myself.

I found myself looking away from Kuru so as not to betray my thoughts on this subject. I didn't care much for his scrutiny. Those dark, quick eyes were a bit daunting to me; I felt that he could see inside me if he chose. As I looked away, I was aware of him brandishing his sword. His gesture wasn't particularly menacing, but rather served to underscore the challenge in his words to me. The challenge prompted an angry response to rise to my lips, but it seemed that he wanted me to rise to his bait, on some level, and so I bit it back with some difficulty. Brawling with a Dragon Knight, especially when I so desperately longed to be one among their order, didn't seem like a particularly helpful idea . . . no matter how provoking the knight.

With an effort, I turned my attention back to my surroundings. I studied the building, which had a number of gears on its wall, and realized with a growing sense of excitement that the faerie woman's cog might well find its place here. Kuru was still pacing the courtyard behind me. In truth, I do not know whether he was watching me or not. I stepped right up to the wall, and put the cog I held on it, back into the empty place where it undoubtedly belonged. Was I expecting some great action to take place? If I was, I was sorely disappointed, for nothing special occurred.

Well, I thought, looking around and trying hard not to let my disappointment show, *that's that*. I felt relieved that I could finally discharge my debt to the motherly faerie lady, and as I remembered her warm smile, a momentary hint of a spring breeze brushed my face, and moved on. As I looked to my right, the wall of the other building had a

peculiarity about it that I wanted to get a closer look at. Upon the wall, faintly outlined in some kind of almost imperceptible magic etching, was a doorway.

Realizing that the most sensible choice available to me was to fight magic with magic, I turned to my Spell Book and realized with a

shock that the kindly sprite had given me a Dispel Illusion spell to add
to my tomes. Since that particular spell seemed to be exactly what was
needed in this instance, I quickly memorized it and cast it at the thin
magic line on the wall, carefully visualizing each magic symbol as
though I were drawing it in the air before me. Gratitude toward that
sprite welled up inside me as the spell worked, and a doorway was
created in front of me, in a wall where there had been no door moments
before. Sneaking a sideways glance at Kuru before I entered this
doorway, I really couldn't tell whether he was watching me with an
expression of disdain or of dawning respect. But at least he was
watching me.

Straightening my shoulders, I marched down the long stone passageway to the forking passages at its other end. On a whim, I decided to bear to the left, and I went down this stone passageway until I reached the door at its end. To my distinct surprise, this door opened into yet another long passage, stone all around like the rest, which branched off to the right and to the left at its end. This was quickly getting confusing. I continued my method of taking the left fork, and found myself at a door which wouldn't open. Now what? As I searched around the walls for some hidden device with which to open it, and considered touching my Dragon Ring to it, as well as other similar fruitless notions, I suddenly remembered the faerie key. The white-haired old faerie woman had given me a key, saying, "this key opens a door in a tunnel not far from here. . . ." From the looks of it, this was that tunnel, and this door the very door she had mentioned.

I was about to fit it into the latch when I heard the other, gentler faerie woman's voice so clearly I turned around, thinking she was standing behind me in the tunnel: ". . . and don't listen to anything my sister tells you." Of course there was no one but me there, standing somewhat sheepishly in front of the door while the hundredfold perfumes of spring enveloped me for a split second before fading away. And then the moment had passed, and I was alone in a stale-smelling tunnel, holding a key that was never meant to be used by my hand.

I turned around, and went slowly back down the corridor until I reached the place where it forked and went off to the left. Whatever was meant for me in this labyrinth, I would find it, without the help of evil white-haired faeries.

The confusing series of hallway upon hallway finally took me to another fork, where I went again to the left. This time, I entered a peculiar room which was dimly lit, with an ornate red-patterned floor. There was another oddly etched door in the wall, but I had more

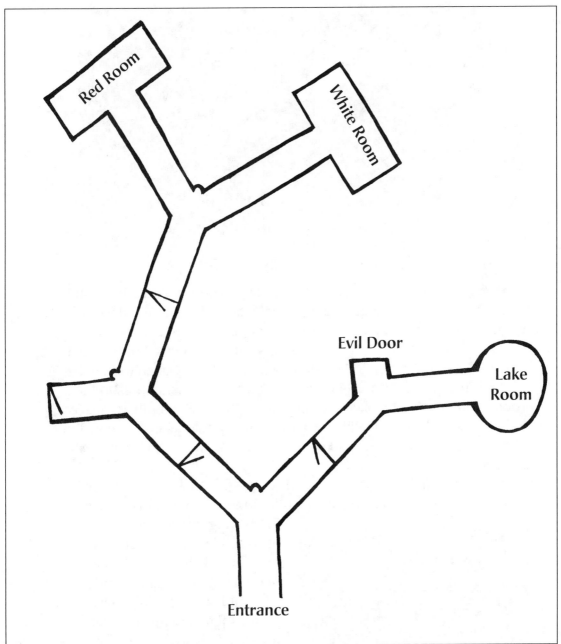

The Labyrinth

exploring to do among these stone hallways before I would have any interest in a door like this. For all I knew, once through the door, I might not have been able to return to this place again, and I was interested in the other rooms in this labyrinth. I promised myself that I would eventually return to this door, and focused my attention on the odd red room. As I looked about, I saw a few odd sculptures in the room, and decided to take a closer look at them. One of them proved to be an upside-down bucket on a pole that I could take. Confused but always on the lookout for useful objects, I took the bucket along with me and left the room.

At the fork in the stone corridor, I went again to the left and this time entered an elaborate room with a white-floored room. There was a

torch lying on the floor, which I hastened to pick up before it went out. Extra lighting was quite a boon amid these dim corridors. Ah, but I was not alone here! A curious figure with a cat-like face (or was it owlish?) and a long striped tail waylaid me the moment I came into the room. Was it man? Was it beast? I could not be sure.

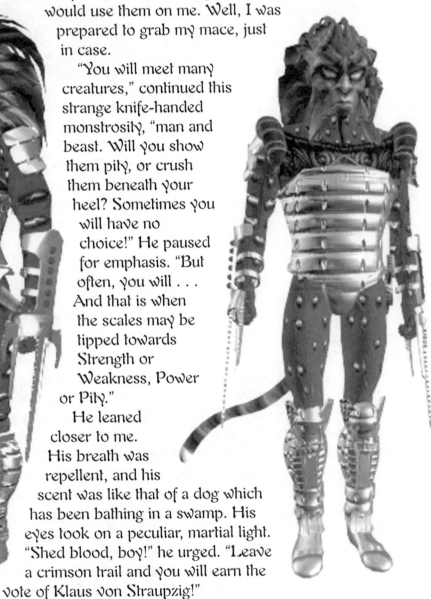

"If you go to the Dolmens, boy, you won't see me!" This was said firmly. "A Dragon Knight wields Power and you wield Pity!"

His strident tones failed to impress me with any sense of wonder or respect. He had the most frightening knives where his hands should have been. I had to respect those. I was beginning to wonder if he would use them on me. Well, I was prepared to grab my mace, just in case.

"You will meet many creatures," continued this strange knife-handed monstrosity, "man and beast. Will you show them pity, or crush them beneath your heel? Sometimes you will have no choice!" He paused for emphasis. "But often, you will . . . And that is when the scales may be tipped towards Strength or Weakness, Power or Pity."

He leaned closer to me. His breath was repellent, and his scent was like that of a dog which has been bathing in a swamp. His eyes took on a peculiar, martial light. "Shed blood, boy!" he urged. "Leave a crimson trail and you will earn the vote of Klaus von Straupzig!"

And that is when the scales may be tipped towards Strength or Weakness, Power or Pity. Shed blood, boy! Leave a crimson trail and you will earn the vote of Klaus von Straupzig!

All this talk of violence and gore was beginning to trouble me. Had I truly chosen the right path? Suddenly it seemed that the more violent of the Dragon Knights were rather pointed in their efforts to redirect my actions. Were they trying to tell me something? What if those who leaned toward violence outnumbered those who didn't? What then of my chosen course of honor and self-respect?

Even as I asked myself these questions, I heard again the earnest voice of Chen Lai, urging me to stay on a path of Wisdom, and saw in my mind the integrity shining from the eyes of Formar Thain and Chelhydra as they encouraged me to stay on that same path. I re-experienced the rush of pride I'd felt upon learning that I would join the ranks of these noble people, were I to prove myself a worthy Dragon Knight.

Strengthening my inner resolve to maintain my personal integrity and avoid senseless brutality, I stalked out of the room without bothering to respond to Klaus. I had actions to pursue of far greater import than listening to a Dragon Knight forcefully expound upon a point of view with which I was never likely to agree in my heart. In my haste to avoid any further discussion with Klaus, I didn't really notice which way I went as I left the white-floored room. I was left to the mercy of the labyrinthine hallways. Left turns were my guides by now, and before I knew it I was facing another door at the end of a long hallway.

This door at least opened freely to me, and I went along the passageway which lay behind it. There, I faced an alcove straight ahead of me, with another passage to my right. Walking along this passageway, I saw a doorway which was filled with luminous blue light. As I got closer to it, I realized that the whole room was reflecting this strange but beautiful blue light. There were plants growing down from the ceiling. The sound of water drops and the faintly fishy odor that our pond used to get toward the end of the summer led me to realize that the effervescent ceiling above me was more than mere illusion — it was naught else but an upside-down lake!

There seemed to be some sense, now, to my having collected the bucket from the red-floored room. I ignored the well on the ground altogether. Taking the bucket, I held it up to the watery ceiling and it was filled with water in precious little time, indeed. It appeared that there was nothing further for me to accomplish in this damp room, so I left it and retraced my steps, always bearing to the left. In this way, I reached the original hallway of this maze of stone passages, and went back out into the sunny courtyard.

I went immediately over to the wall with the gears, as something inside told me that this bucketful of lake water was a potential tool. As I stood in front of the gears, I noticed something I had failed to see before — there was a small handle, sticking out from the wall, directly

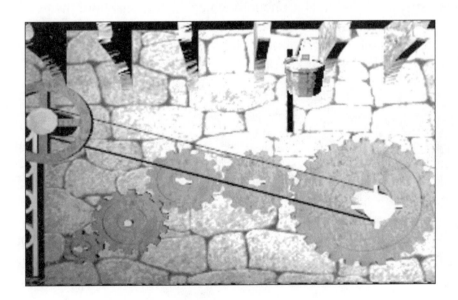

above those cogs. Without even stopping to analyze my actions, I stepped up onto my tiptoes and managed to hang the bucket on that handle. As the water poured from the lever onto the gears, they began to squeak and turn and squeak some more, and the gated door off to the side was pulled open by the force of their turning!

I ran into the doorway, and was dismayed to find a simple set of stairs leading up to a room. The room was quite simple as well, and its only contents were a large plank with two chests on it. The chest in front of me was the one I wanted to take; it appeared from the precarious position of the plank that I could choose only one, as the other would then fall down. The door on the other side of the room

looked suspiciously like the one into which I had nearly put the evil key. I was fairly certain that the chest on that side of the room was not intended for use by a man of noble intent, and so I had little interest in it. Taking the chest which lay directly in front of me, I left this room and

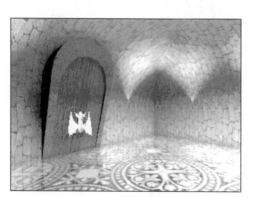

re-entered the labyrinth, intent upon finding the red-floored room once more. Now that I had seen all there was to see here, and put myself in possession of this chest, I wanted to find out what was behind that secret door.

The red room's secret door opened into a small stone hallway. At the end of the hall, there was a

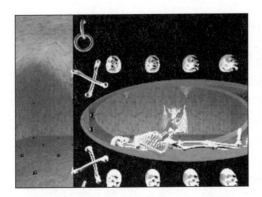
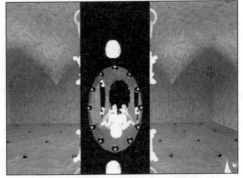

stone room, which contained an elaborately fashioned black coffin, covered with bones and skulls. I walked further into the room, appreciating the hushed silence around me, and the dim lighting. The sight of these Dragon Knight burials was one to which I was rapidly becoming accustomed. The contents of the crypt — a skeleton — commanded a certain amount of my respect and attention. Its hands were held with the palms upright, as though it were waiting to hold something significant. This is a special room, I thought, because this was a special man. The entire room seemed to contain an anticipatory air, as though yearning for some kind of final act or statement or gesture which would let it rest peacefully in its darkened silence. Something here had been left undone. I felt this in my bones, and yet I was uncertain as to what was expected from me.

I racked my brain to imagine what could be needed in this place. My Dragon Ring, I was certain, was not the answer here. Mentally, I retraced the recent steps I'd made, through the labyrinth of hallways and the peculiar room in the building with the cogs. I had picked up a chest when there was a choice of two. I had chosen the chest from the side which did not conform to the evil key the cruel faerie had given me. As I thought of the chest, the hair on the back of my neck stood up. Taking it out of my pack to look closely at it, I realized that there was no way to open it. Finally, because it seemed to be

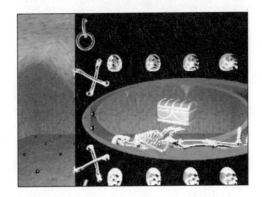

the appropriate gesture, I took the chest I'd found in the cog building, and set it upon the open hands of the skeleton. Although I wasn't particularly squeamish, I set the case down carefully, not wanting to touch the bones of the skeleton accidentally.

The effect of this action was startling. The entire crypt quivered and creaked, and fell down through the floor with a rumble. Before I had time enough to blink, it came rumbling back up. There was a small shining object on the top of it which turned out to be a ring. I took it, and then heard the voice of the long-dead Fujitomo.

"You have given me back my soul. The curse is lifted at last," the voice breathed. "Now I may rest in peace! You will have the vote of Fujitomo!"

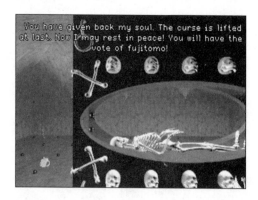
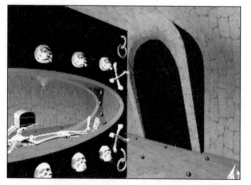

This, then, was the ring of Fujitomo! I exhaled deeply, releasing breath that I'd been holding for I knew not how long. Now I was assured Fujitomo's vote, so long as I held his ring. I slipped it into a safe place, concealing it from the danger of inquiring eyes.

There was a pitch-black doorway on the other side of the room. As I looked into it, I saw only nothingness. Because I was certain that this was the direction in which I was to go next, I held my torch high above my head and stepped into the blackened door.

Herg nach Drakhonen

Harsh daylight greeted my eyes on the other side of the black door. The contrast was so severe, compared to the darkness from which I had just emerged, that I was unable to focus for a moment on my new surroundings, and I just stood there, blinking and rubbing my eyes. As the mountainous area around me and the cobblestones upon which I stood came into focus, so did the wild-eyed, red-haired man pacing around in front of me. Because he was armed to the teeth, my impression was that this was yet another violent Dragon Knight ready to goad me into violent and ill-considered action. *How many more of these knights are there?* I wondered with a sigh.

As I hailed this fierce-looking stranger, I resigned myself to the inevitable lecture about my weak habits and lack of bloodlust.

"Just kill the pike, lad! On the other hand, you could let him swallow you, but getting out again might be tricky!" The suspicion

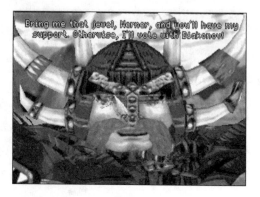

that this man was not only violent, but a lunatic as well, crossed my mind. What was a pike, anyhow? Was this a joke of some sort?

"I am Herg nach Drakhonen, and I'll be voting . . . that is, if you get as far as your election." He grinned a crooked grin. "Wisdom and Violence, Order and Chaos. They are just words for me, Werner. I care little how intelligent or how brutal you are!"

I couldn't have been more surprised by Herg's blatant indifference to the question of Wisdom versus Force. He simply didn't care. He interrupted my musings by saying, "But if you want my vote. . .You'll soon come across the only Duck Dragon left alive in the world."

I had never heard of a Duck Dragon, and told him so. He shrugged his shoulders at my ignorance. "A fabulous beast, Werner! It collects precious stones, of all kinds. It especially covets diamonds; they hypnotize the creature!" Herg's voice began to take on a lunatic edge; he was becoming hysterical as he reached the climax of this monologue. "The furnace of the Duck Dragon's breath melts all its jewels together to make a single stone, the most magnificent jewel there is! Bring me that jewel, Werner, and you'll have my support. Otherwise, I'll vote with Diakonov!"

Taken aback by his avarice, I was nonetheless profoundly relieved that I was spared another diatribe on the subject of violence. But who was Diakonov?

Duck dragons and fabulous gems sounded intriguing to me. Besides, although Herg's disdain for the agendas of his fellow Dragon Knights shocked me, his honesty was engaging, and I liked him. Furthermore, I wanted his vote. It sounded fairly simple — get a gem for him, get his vote. No strings, no long-term consequences to contend with. No problem.

The River

My confidence level was pretty high as I walked along the path through the mountainous area. Little hills and rocky passes came and went as I wended my way down to the banks of the river. Briefly, I wondered if this were the same river I'd crossed with the ferry, earlier. As I looked around for bridges or rafts or anything I could use to cross this river with, my search turned up nothing. It looked as though swimming across was the only real option. Fortunately, I had learned to swim in our pond when I was a small boy, so this wasn't as intimidating a prospect to me as it could have been. Hoping that I wouldn't lose any of my hard-won possessions, I jumped into the water and swam for the other side. Once under the water, I was relieved it wasn't as icy as it looked. It was nippy enough, though, and I wasn't looking forward to freezing on the bank once I got out, still clad in sodden clothes. My musings on this were curtailed abruptly,

however, by the sight of an enormous fish coming straight at me! There wasn't time enough to find a weapon; besides my clothes were heavy and the going was slow enough as it was. I tried feebly to outswim the fish, but it was upon me before I knew it, its huge maw opening upon me. And then I was in an appallingly smelly, airless little space, the sides of which were sticky and oozing. I realized with a start that I was inside the belly of an overgrown minnow! Herg's words, insensibly, came back to me at this opportune moment — "Unless he swallows you . . ." — and I realized that this creature must be a pike.

As I picked around between the bits of partially digested fish and other river creatures in my efforts to devise some solution to freeing

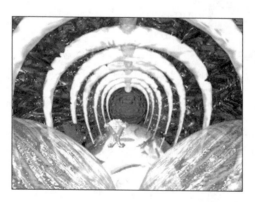

myself from this fishy prison, I saw a magnificent sparkling stone on the floor. As I picked it up, the diamond reflected what little light there was inside the pike. Although I had no use for such a beautiful gem right now, I knew it would come in handy when I met the Duck Dragon, so I pocketed it. I scratched my head, and looked around a bit more. How was I going to get out of this one? I scratched absently at my back while I paced about in the limited space afforded by this pike's belly. I scratched. In fact, I was beginning to itch a lot all over, so I wanted to get out of here quickly, before I managed to scratch my skin off. Even the inside of my ears and nose itched. Dreading another sneezing attack, I rubbed my nose vigorously.

This action caused me to remember the yellow flowers I still had in my possession. They had made me want to sneeze when I'd first encountered them. It seemed almost logical for me to hold one of them in my hand and tickle the ribs of the gigantic fish with it. And sure enough, in a giant paroxysm of quivering flesh, I was sneezed right out of the pike's sticky belly and thrown through the water, up and out, right into the air. I landed in a heap on the riverbank, exactly at the place I'd been aiming for when I first dove into the water. The brief contact with the river on my way out of it served to rinse off my itchy skin, so I felt pretty good, and not even all that smelly. I picked myself up off the ground and studied the walls of the cavern-like arch in front of me. Veering off to the left, I began to walk briskly through the rock formations there, hoping that my rapid pace would warm me up sufficiently. Perhaps my clothes could even dry a bit.

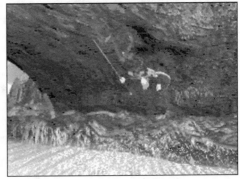

As I picked my way around the rocks, the roaring sound of rushing water met my ears. I continued my precarious footwork amid the loose and sometimes pointy rocks. Finally, I came upon a beautiful, flourishing willow tree which stood on the side of a clear pond. The rushing water was now so thunderous that I was unable to hear my own

footsteps. I went to the willow, and walked up to the side of the pond. There was a rough path of sorts, just below me, so I jumped down to it and then walked toward the crashing water. As I neared the source of the noise, a huge waterfall, I noticed a clearing just behind the water. There was a place between the rocks and the waterfall where no water was, and I was able to walk right into it, without getting any wetter from the spray than I already was. The clear place opened into a giant cave, deep and dark and filled with sparkling stones. They pointed up from

all angles and down from the ceiling. The effect of all the light they cast was magnificent, a hundred times more powerful than the sunshine reflecting from our frosted fields in the wintertime, and just as pure.

In the middle of all of this splendour trod the Duck Dragon. He was by far the smallest dragon I had yet encountered, and he made a curious

sound, much like the chattering of a duck. I was at something of a loss. The Duck Dragon wouldn't respond to my greetings; indeed, he more or less ignored me as he wandered aimlessly around among his stones.

In a fit of inspiration, I pulled out the diamond I'd found in the

pike's stomach, hoping it didn't reek too much of fish. I held it out in front of me as an offering to the Duck Dragon. In his ramblings, which I had considered to be no more than the delusions of a pleasant lunatic, Herg had mentioned that the Duck Dragon was hypnotized by diamonds. This certainly seemed to be the case, for the Duck Dragon was unaccountably drawn to the diamond I held out, and gently took it from me as if in a daze. He then turned and slowly waddled back into his den, and I followed the bewildered creature until he indicated that I could pick up the stone in his beak. It was so extraordinarily beautiful that I was certain it was the very one craved by Herg. I took the stone from the Duck Dragon, and quickly made my exit through the waterfall. I hastened to leave before the creature changed its mind.

Once outside, I scaled the little hill that had brought me to this place, and turned away from the willow to retrace my steps until I reached the river. At the bank again, I calmly dove into the cold water once more and swam across to the other side. Mercifully, the pike did not attack me this time.

Upon my return to the courtyard, Herg was still there, anxiously rubbing his hands together and muttering under his breath. When I wordlessly gave him the gem, his eyes glazed over with the fire of obsession, and he began to rave about the bauble as though it were the apex of his

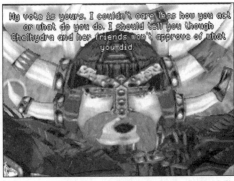

existence. "I have it! The dream of a lifetime, here in my hand," he cried, his voice straining into higher registers than I had thought possible. Suddenly, Herg seemed transformed to an earlier age, appearing and sounding like a youth. How long had he lusted after this jewel? Since his youth? He turned it over and over again, staring at the facets of the stone, catching light rays in it.

After a few minutes of this, I cleared my throat. Herg broke himself away from his absorption in his gem, and with an obvious effort seemed to recall my presence. "My vote is yours." He spoke solemnly. "I couldn't care less how you act or what you do. I should tell you, though — Chelhydra and her friends won't approve of what you did."

I shrugged. Certainly, I was pleased to have won his vote by bringing him the gem, although a bit chagrined to hear that Chelhydra wouldn't be as content as I was with this choice of mine. "What's done is done," I replied softly, fully intending to proceed along my journey as honorably and courageously as I could. If Chelhydra wasn't thoroughly happy right now, well, she would come around again. After all, I could only perform to the best of my ability.

As I left Herg, he was still lost in his fanatical admiration of the precious stone I had brought him. Once again, I crossed through the rocks and went down to the river. As I jumped in to swim back across it, the pike chased me once more and swallowed me again. Fortunately, experience is a wonderful teacher, so I was spared the sensation of my skin crawling; I didn't have to inhale the effluvium of the pike's rotting breakfast for very long, either. I merely tickled the pikey ribs with my remaining yellow flower and crouched down in preparation for my turns through the air. In truth, the landing wasn't any easier than it had been the first time; I still crumpled up in a heap on the river bank.

Heleynea d'Artica

Back at the willow tree near the waterfall, I jumped down the side of the pond again, and leapt from stone to stone, across the end of the pond.

As I reached the other side, I had to scramble a bit to climb up onto the bank, and then I faced some beautiful trees. As I walked past them, the noise from the falls abated, and I came into a colder, mountainous area,

 with towering hills somewhat reminiscent of the mountains around my home. I found a path leading up through some dolmen-like arches, and trudged up and up and up. The circular motion made me a trifle dizzy as I went along. Curiosity about what was at the top of all of this kept me going until I reached the top of the

mountain. I was looking over the edges of what appeared to be an ancient citadel, and as I took a step or two into the circle of stones, an odd flapping sound from the air above caused me to look up.

There was a dragon . . . flying above the citadel. Never had I seen a creature its equal. It was massive, with translucent wings and a long, graceful neck. I marveled at the power and suppleness of the winged beast, envious of its rider — for there, atop the creature, rode a woman. She appeared to guide the powerful beast without effort. The motion of the dragon was so smooth that it appeared as if dragon and rider acted as a single being. At first, it seemed that the dragon would fly right past the citadel, but it approached the structure and came gently to a halt on one of the stone arches.

The rider, a stunning Dragon Knight, was a very young woman dressed in battle clothes. She was barely a maiden, much younger even than Tanathya. I wasn't sure that she was any older than I was! As she slipped fluidly off of the dragon's back, it was obvious that she was little and lithe, but possessed of great physical strength. The blue outfit she wore seemed effervescent in the gray light. Her battle helmet bespoke a serious personality, prepared for any contingency. This young maid was not afraid of anything!

When she faced me, I was keenly aware of staring into the most vital pair of eyes I'd ever seen, though set in such a forbidding expression! A proud, somewhat distant Dragon Knight, she greeted me with a cold ferocity. "If you are not the son of Axel von Wallenrod, then turn

Prove to me who you are.

He won't break the Pact of Peace, since we're not enemies! Our two families have been allies for many generations. A friendly duel, that's all I'm suggesting. Either of us may end it by throwing down their weapon!

around and leave. I, Heleynea of the House of d'Artica, have sworn to let none but Werner von Wallenrod past this place!"

Then, the Lady Heleynea looked me straight in the eye, fingering her mighty sword and demanded, "Prove to me who you are!" What did she mean, prove to her? Was not my presence here proof enough? Although outraged, I kept my ire to myself and presented the von Wallenrod Dragon Ring for her inspection.

As she inspected the ring, she told me, "Your father was a brave and just knight. He could not wish his son to be any different." Was. There, then, was confirmation of the vague suspicions I'd had along this journey. My father was dead. It was his ring I carried. I doubted that a maid this young could have known my father, but I kept this reflection private, as well. The next words of Heleynea startled me greatly. "We won't break the Pact of Peace, since we're not enemies! Our two families have been allies for many generations." This was obviously news to me. My jaw was hanging open. But what was she getting at?

"A friendly duel, that's all I'm suggesting. Either of us may end it by throwing down their weapon!" Was this serious? Her challenge created a great conflict in me. Was I supposed to attack a woman? Dragon Knight or no Dragon Knight, Heleynea was a lady, and I'd never heard of any nobleman dueling with a young maid. It didn't seem right, especially if she was a kinswoman, of a sort.

Yet, if our families were really that close, perhaps this kind of fighting was commonplace among their members. A matter of honor, or some such tradition. I didn't know anything about the

customs of my own family. It seemed that this was the time for me to learn. These conflicting thoughts and feelings flitted through me in a matter of seconds. I didn't have the time to dwell on them, really, or to sort them out into any order that made sense to me, for Heleynea had drawn steel — not one sword but two! — and really meant to strike at me! "You'll have my vote if you continue to act with honor," she exclaimed breathily.

Though I had my mace in hand, I didn't know how seriously to take all this talk of challenges and mettle, until Heleynea thrust at me with her swords and sliced part of my arm open. I could only stare at the blood gushing out of me like some red waterfall. Stunned, for I really hadn't thought she would hurt me, I reacted with ferocity and swung the mace

with all of my strength until I got a good hit in on her. The moment I saw blood welling up under her breastplate, I was horrified, but she didn't seem the least fazed by it and in fact nailed me again, this time delivering a much more painful wound to my side. Confused and in pain, I felt a momentary anger and wanted to rip her to shreds.

In my next conscious thought, though, I realized that I must not act upon this anger. I couldn't have lived with myself had I struck at Heleynea again, out of my rage, so I threw down my weapon. As I did so, it occurred to me that this would appear to be a cowardly act on my part, as if I had been bested by this girl. But, on second thought, I really didn't care. Holding my side and feeling the warm blood — my blood, I thought savagely — trickle over my fingers, I faced Heleynea and stared directly into her eyes.

To my amazement, she was smiling. "Your father would be proud of your courage, Werner von Wallenrod. You may throw down your weapon with honor." I felt the bleeding stop, suddenly and inexplicably. Heleynea's garments were clean once more.

Completely stunned yet again — it was becoming a habit around this young warrior — I listened as Heleynea expressed my own ideas about courage versus brutality — to me! "You are truly a man of honour, Werner," she proclaimed. "You know the difference between courage and brutality. You can count on my vote."

It was as though she had heard the inner dialogue I'd been having with myself ever since this journey started. Her articulation of the credo written in my own heart, exactly as I felt it, caused me to feel related to Heleynea in a way that I had never experienced in my entire life. Perhaps the bond that our families had shared was responsible for our similarity of outlook on these matters; I did not know or care. I was awash in the joy of discovering that I was not alone.

"I've healed you with a spell, Werner. You'll need all of your strength for the castle." And it was true, not only had the bleeding from my side

and arm ceased, but I felt rested and alert, as I had at the beginning of this adventure. She very kindly gave me a pickax that I was to use once in some dangerous place, warned me about the struggles I would face in trying to reach the castle, and then she was, much to my disappointment, gone.

The wind at the top of the citadel grew suddenly cold with her absence. I lingered awhile, perhaps hoping she would return, but I knew in my heart that it was not to be. I would not see Heleynea again until she cast her vote for me, and that was all there was to it. Finally, I could bear the frigid wind no more, and I made my way back down the spiraling path, pondering my sudden heights of joy and depths of despondency as I went. Once at the bottom of the hill, I walked around it until I returned to the main road which had brought me here, and I turned as it turned, to head straight into the mountains.

Eventually, I came upon a place in the path where it was blocked by many fallen rocks. The blockage looked like the result of an avalanche, and had it not been for the pickax given me by Heleynea, I never would have made it through. As it was, it took me a long time to break up the rocks enough so that I could pass through them. The whole time I chopped, I thought about what Heleynea had said about our families being close.

I was still having difficulty considering myself a von Wallenrod. I didn't really know what it meant, aside from being a Dragon Knight and observing a creed of honor. Everyone kept telling me to go to the castle, and although it was obviously my destination, I couldn't imagine what it would be like. It just didn't seem real to me. The idea that the Castle von Wallenrod was my rightful home didn't make any sense to me, so I didn't waste much time thinking about that.

Haagen von Diakonov

Finally, the rocks were broken up and I crossed through them without any difficulty, leaving the dulled pickax by the roadside as I went on. I came into a darker clearing, surrounded by craggy mountains, which looked as though it had been subject to many of nature's torments. An

enormous tree loomed on my right, a tree that appeared to have been struck repeatedly by lightning or some other blight. It appeared to be completely dead, with no branches, no leaves, no life anywhere. There was a stream here, too, but it ran muddy, dirty and brown, entirely unlike any of the other streams I had encountered along my travels. I couldn't see any way to cross it, either, and the prospect of splashing through that murky brown water was most unappetizing. All in all, this was a gloomy and depressing setting. Small wonder that the horrible black figure should be waiting here for me.

With my mace in my hand and my teeth gritted, for I had not forgotten the last time our paths had crossed, I approached the dark knight with murder in my heart. He was evidently not in any mood to fight me himself, but seemed more interested in toying with me, as a cat toys with a mouse. His disdain for me was writ all over his face.

"Stuck again?" The very question was an insult. "You know who I am, don't you?"

He paused for dramatic effect. "Haagen von Diakonov, Dragon Knight," said he, bowing ironically," which is something you'll never be, farmboy!" I did not return his bow, merely kept my jaw clenched shut.

"Even if you get as far as the election, and believe me, you won't, you can't hope to win," he continued in a polished tone, "so take my advice: give up while you have the chance! Run back to your farm. Daisy's so lonely without you!" His taunts, although farfetched and distorted, stung a bit. I refused to let him see how sensitive I was in the face of his scorn, though I felt my face flush. I turned to go.

"Oh, farmboy!" His hateful accents brought me spinning around, angrily. "I've decided to give you an ax to cut down the old tree. It should've been done long ago, but your ancestors were sentimental!" And with that, Haagen gave me his ax, and vanished before I could have the satisfaction of wielding it against him.

Distrusting his motivations, I wrestled with my conscience, considered carrying the evil thing to the muddied waters of the creek and throwing it in. Did I really want to use this ax? How did I know that chopping the tree down was a good idea? Perhaps he was deliberately trying to mislead me, and induce me to do something that ultimately would harm me, or my family name. Or perhaps he was trying to test me in some way. There was no way to be sure. I realized in a flash that the greatest part of my travels entailed risk, and it was up to me to answer the challenges of fate accordingly. The road to adventure left little room for hesitation.

I stepped up to the huge, ancient tree trunk, swallowed my reservations about felling it, and proceeded to chop it down. Finally, my only doubts left were those about which way the great tree would fall. I certainly hoped it would end up in such a way as to afford me a crossing of the stream. And it did. Before I crossed the stream by crawling across the tree trunk, I decided to leave Haagen's ax behind.

Shuddering at the thought of what awful deeds it must have been used to perpetrate, I had no desire to carry such a vile weapon. And I didn't even know the half of it, then.

The Two Thieves

Once I crossed the stream, I came across a sparsely wooded area, edged all around with the dark mountains that were beginning to seem familiar to me. This country, though desolate in some ways, was mystically beautiful in others. I was developing an appreciation for these craggy, misty landscapes. Wrapped up in my thoughts, I continued along until I heard voices and saw two highly unsavory characters coming toward me. Although they looked dirty and suspicious — and armed — I hadn't encountered anyone except von Diakonov who'd wished me ill along my travels. My desire was not to judge their appearance, but rather to see of what help these two could be to me along my quest.

"What have we got here, Heine?" the little masked faced dwarf, by far the shorter of the two, demanded of his partner as I approached them.

The partner, a horned creature, sniffed the air around me. By way of response, Heine, this strapping green goblin, stated with a question in his voice, "Looks like he's lost, Herman?" I was about to interrupt and explain myself, but they just went right on talking about me as if I weren't even there!

Herman replied, "Yeah, but he's a smart little fellow. He made a nice bridge just for us."

Heine the troll giggled. "And we're grateful, right, Herman?"

In a knowing chuckle which certainly couldn't be interpreted as anything other than a threat, Herman replied, "We certainly are, Heine. And we'll be even gratefuler when he gives us all those lovely things he's carrying!"

Thieves? Thieves!?!! I couldn't believe my ears. Did these two imbeciles have any idea who they were dealing with? At this point in my journey, I was an experienced fighter who carried the Dragon Ring of the von Wallenrods. Indeed, I was nearly a Dragon Knight! How dare they assume they could rob me? It was preposterous.

"He'd better hurry up and hand everything over or we'll have to kill him dead." My mace was out before Herman even finished this sentence. I sincerely believed it would be the last he'd ever utter. The shocked expression on the faces of the two thieves as I came running at them, mace flying wildly through the air, a heated flush on my face brought on by a mixture of sudden anger and exhilaration, told me that they agreed with my belief. Though I had not yet contended with two

men at once, I was full of confidence that the task of ending their lives would not be an overly trying one. Furious at their presumption that I was some innocent victim to be plucked by them, like some prone chicken, I slashed and hacked at them until they collapsed upon one another in a sorry, colorless heap on the ground.

I had barely broken a sweat, so frenzied was I to be rid of such criminals. Grimly, I surveyed the sight of them. There was no remorse whatsoever in my heart, and I fell on one knee to search through their belongings. I did not suffer thieves and knaves gladly. No doubt everything I found had been stolen from other hapless travelers along this path.

The search proved fruitful. I found a beautiful sword, though I wondered by what means they had wrested it from its owner. There were also a wooden staff and a burlap sack. The staff would come in handy crossing through these mountains, it seemed to me. As I opened the bag, shards of fine broken porcelain fell out of it, nearly shredding my fingers as they tumbled. I peered into the bag, and saw that there were two vases in it. One was in fine form, pleasing to look at and obviously well-crafted. The other one, although it had probably once been as attractive as this vase, was broken past repair. I took both vases out of the sack, moving carefully for fear of being cut on the shards of the broken one. In an effort to protect the unbroken vase, I cleared the shards of glass out of the sack as best I could, then wrapped the vase in the thick folds of the burlap, so that I could carry it without damaging it. The broken vase I simply left there on the ground, having little use for it.

Sylvan and Alexander

I walked toward the mountains, and upon reaching them, found a place where two of them separated, making a pass of sorts for me to take through them. I followed it until I reached a great courtyard, larger than any I had seen before. This was a most magnificent place. Benches and columns were scattered around the cobblestoned floor, and a stone-walled pond filled with clear water sparkled off to one side. There was even a small island of a sort, in the middle of the pond.

Off in the distance were stone archways which resembled aqueducts, and farther beyond them were the dark spires of an enormous structure, silhouetted

against the mountains. With a jolt of excitement, I realized that those spires belonged to a castle. The Castle von Wallenrod! It must be! In my joy at seeing what I believed to be the home I sought, and the journey's end, I was slow to notice that I was not alone in this elegant courtyard.

When I finally became aware of the odd — well, was it a person? I couldn't really decide — creature coming toward me, it was so a bizarre a sight that it startled me quite a bit. What I saw was almost impossible to describe. There was a man, but taller than any man, with two heads, one where his head ought to have been, and one in his stomach. Or was that the shoulders of the other? I could not determine this. There were four arms on this unnatural piece of work, all armed with small

battle-axes. And it walked about on two legs, elegantly dressed and impeccably balanced. It was the elegance garb which dispelled my caution; I had feared that these were more thieves, come to rob me. This figure, whatever it was, was no thief.

Although the flailing battle-axes were a bit daunting, I wanted very much to know if I'd arrived at the Castle von Wallenrod, so I walked right up to this bizarre freak and asked it so. Asked *them* so. Totally ignoring my question as though it were the prattling of a child, the properly placed head addressed me.

"Werner von Wallenrod, I am Sylvan of Sygill!" Sylvan's face was long and his eyes were dark slits, but his demeanor was courtly and he wore a blue velvet hat. It reminded me of the iridescent colour worn by Heleynea.

"And I," chimed the lower head, "am Alexander of Egregalion. You need votes, if you want to join the Brotherhood of Dragon Knights!" Alexander was also narrow of face and features, though his face was covered in some mystical black markings that I was unable to decipher.

I was never more shocked than the moment I discovered that these two — for they were two distinct individuals, though they maintained the same torso — were Dragon Knights. Ashamed at my own prejudice, I responded to their greetings in a most civil way.

Sylvan interrupted Alexander, saying, "A vase was stolen from me, by two thieves. You will have my vote if you bring it to me."

And Alexander swiftly explained, "The thieves also stole my vase. The two vases are almost identical. Bring me back my vase, and you'll have my vote."

Oh, now here was a dilemma, indeed! What was I to do? When I tried to explain that I'd indeed come upon those knavish thieves, but only had recovered one of the vases, neither Sylvan nor Alexander would hear a word of it. Each wanted the intact vase for himself, and I was in a quandary as to which one to return it to. Whichever one I returned it to would vote for me, of that much I was certain. Would the other, then, not vote for me? I badly wanted both votes. I sat down on one of the benches to ponder my next course of action. Wearied as I was, with my head aching, it did me good to rest a bit.

As I sat, I tossed it around in my mind. Sylvan or Alexander? Both were fine, ethical knights. I couldn't really go wrong, no matter which one I gave it to. At least, I pondered, I was assured of one vote. It didn't really matter to me, then, which one I gave it to. Except that I wouldn't want to confront the other one! Finally, not knowing what else to do, I closed my eyes, and held out the good vase.

Sylvan snatched it from my hands, saying gleefully as he did so, "You've chosen well, Werner. My vote will be yours."

Alexander, on the other hand, wasn't too philosophical about his loss. "Fool!" he exclaimed. "Can't you tell an honest man from a liar? I hope you don't die in your castle, so I can have the pleasure of watching you lose the election!"

It seemed safe to assume that I was not to have the vote of Alexander. I felt badly, for I liked him a great deal, and didn't enjoy the sight of a great Dragon Knight acting in such a petty fashion. I turned to go, shaking my head. As I walked away, they were still bickering over the ownership of the one good vase.

After traversing the huge courtyard, I continued through the impressive archways, along a long path. It led right up to a flight of stairs — and the stairs led into the Castle von Wallenrod. As I mounted them, two at a time, I wondered what new dangers would be found within the castle. As I went through the gated door, I was elated. I was home! I would be a Dragon Knight at last!

PART TWO: The Castle

The Entry

The stairs leading up to the castle were steep, and as I climbed, I felt a slight weakness in my legs and my breath came in short gulps, though it was not the steepness of the path that so affected me. The wind was picking up, and I shivered as I reached the top of the stairs. The castle seemed awfully quiet. Was there no one to greet me? My spirits were caught up in a strange and unfamiliar mixture of anticipation and fear. Now that I was here, I felt a band across my chest and a grip at the pit of my stomach. In honesty, I was scared of what I would find within the walls of the Castle von Wallenrod. This moment, more than any other foray into the unknown, struck me deeply; this was the threshold of my future. There was truly no returning to the farming life and the blissful ignorance of that world, its peaceful surroundings and uneventful existence. This was my destiny. I was becoming a man, though I had only a vague awareness of my transformation when I walked into the Castle von Wallenrod for the first time.

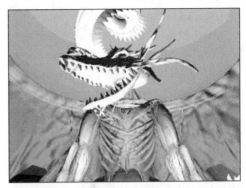

The door in front of me had a sculpture of a dragon's head on it. I pushed it aside firmly as I entered an enormous cave-like room and confronted the most gigantic dragon I had seen yet. The chamber was airless and dense, and I felt that I could scarcely breathe. In the center of the huge round room sat the dragon. In front of it, in the eerie light, was a strangely wrought sculpture. On the top of the sculpture was a giant, luminous sphere. Instinctively, I reached out to touch the glowing orb. It was fascinating, as it seemed to be glowing from within.

The moment I actually tried to touch it, the dragon, which until this point had kept as still as a magnificently crafted statue, leaned down

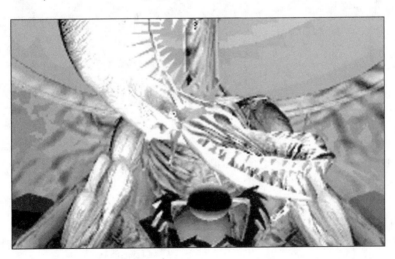

from its Olympian height and roared at me, its red eyes flashing. As its breath touched the sphere, the strange orb glowed bright orange and red. I was momentarily frozen in place. Had I not been, I would most certainly have run back out the way I had come. If this was the castle's guardian dog, then Brutus and Schatzie had been more like guardian mice.

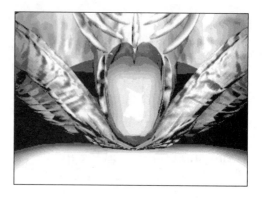

The dragon returned to its statue-like vigil. Moments later, when I could move, and I realized that I had not been incinerated (or worse) by the dragon, I backed off and searched for a way out of this cave. As I walked slowly around the room, not wishing to rouse the great creature's ire any more than I had already done, I discovered the way out. It lay directly between the dragon's legs. Sweating and holding my breath, I tiptoed delicately out the door. To my relief, the dragon did not stir again.

As I left the cave, I stepped immediately onto a wooden drawbridge, its enormous chains reaching up to the castle walls. I studied the portcullis entrance ahead, whilst shivering from the sharp contrast in temperature between the warm, airless cave and this outside bridge over the craggy cliffs. A smallish green dragon stood solemnly before me, much weathered and scarred. This dragon bore an astonishing resemblance to the one I had encountered early on in my travels, the one in the tomb under the Dolmens. This type of guardian was at least not unknown to me. I greeted him shyly, as I was still unaccustomed to dealing with dragons, and he responded at once, asking me, "By what right do you trouble those who dwell in this castle?"

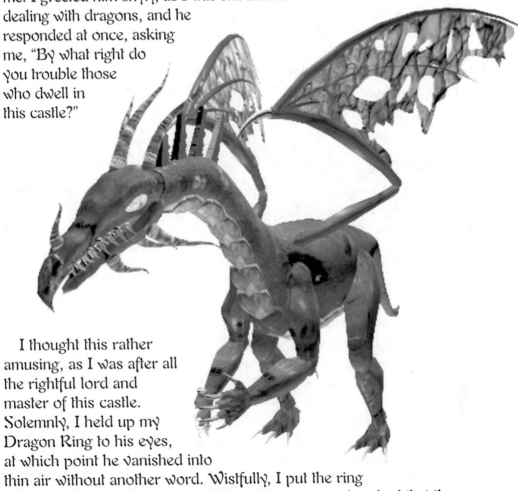

I thought this rather amusing, as I was after all the rightful lord and master of this castle. Solemnly, I held up my Dragon Ring to his eyes, at which point he vanished into thin air without another word. Wistfully, I put the ring back on my finger. I was quite fond of dragons, and wished that they wouldn't all act so aloof or disappear so quickly.

The Throne Room

And so I passed through the portcullis, eager to get on with it all. The room which met my wondering gaze was vast, much larger than any I had previously encountered. The floors and ceilings were hewn from the finest marble, polished so it shone brightly. There were more sculptures of dragons than I could count; some of them stood as high as the ceilings, while others were my own height. Dragons, dragons everywhere. Oh, this had been the home of a Dragon Knight, make no doubt. Light streaming in from the windows illuminated a huge yellow W, inlaid in the floor. The very top of the W pointed to an elaborate throne of some carved stone, at the far end of the room.

There were numerous doorways to investigate, but as I advanced into the airy room, I spied a creature, a thing, an undead yellow wretch that walked about the room, armed to the teeth and clearly wanting to clash with me. It gave, to all appearances, the air of a creature protecting its lair, and acted as though I were an intruder.

"How came this evil into my house? Begone, you vile thing!" I spat out, as I pulled forth my mace and looked for a good opening. The creature came at me with a rattling sound, whirling a spiked club at my head. We engaged in combat, and I soon realized that I was matched evenly with this yellow non-man. What's more, I was tiring. I looked around madly for an advantage, a way to hit and not be hit, a ledge, anything that would help me. The stairs underneath the

dragon statues proved to be the most useful. Luring the yellow fighter over to them, I quickly mounted them, then turned on him. From my slightly raised height, I was able to strike at him more often than he was able to hit me, and in this way made quick work of him.

Once I was certain that he was finished, never to rise again, I went straight up to the throne. It was flanked by dragons, and I could easily

envision my father sitting on this throne. I gulped. I would be the next von Wallenrod to occupy that hallowed seat — if I survived, that is. This realization left an empty feeling in my stomach. There was a strange ache in my throat. I should have liked to have known my own father, after all.

I turned abruptly and went to the rear of the hall, taking care not to step anywhere near the carcass on the floor. Facing back toward the door I had used to enter this hallway I noticed an arched doorway to the right. Intrigued, I went through it.

The Chapel

I walked all the way to the very back of the chapel, which was where the arched doorway had led me, along each pew. I wondered how long it had been since this place had last seen a priest of any kind. The chapel had that damp, cloying odor that rooms often get with disuse, yet mixed into it was the faintest hint of incense. At the very end of the stone wall, I came across another arched, wooden doorway and went though it. It creaked a bit as I pushed on it, but opened easily enough.

The Vestry

The deserted vestry filled me with a sense of sadness. Was every room in this place so empty? From the looks of it, since many cabinets were hanging open, their contents entirely visible and sometimes spilt, this room had been ransacked at some time and left in that condition. As I turned to my left, I spied a lectern with a holy book upon it. That much, at least, had not been violated in this sacred space. I pocketed the book, thinking that it would prove useful later.

My sentiments of honor having been violated as I witnessed the disarray in this room, I prowled around in a kind of fascinated horror, peering into the open cabinets and drawers left sorrowfully ajar. I even tried to read the notes of the cleric who'd inhabited this room, hoping to discover some clues to the mysteries surrounding me. He'd left them in a red bound book on the writing table, but they were in an obscure language and I was unable to decipher the words. At the foot of the elaborately carved bed, I found a cabinet which had some candles on it. I collected the candles. I had no idea how many dark crannies I would be exploring in this castle, and the added light would no doubt be necessary.

The Chapel (again)

After another turn around the room, I left it, returning to the chapel. My steps led me to the altar, where I noticed the candelabra at once. It was missing three candles — the same number of candles I'd found in the vestry — and I threw my caution about future dark places to the wind and placed the candles in the empty places on the candelabra. The moment I had done so, a strange secret door in the wooden altar opened! I saw a glitter of gold there, reached in and brought forth a small golden triangle. Examining the artifact, I felt sure it was but part of a larger object, for there was an insignia scribed on it which continued past the edge of the triangle. I promised myself to keep an eye out for other pieces of this golden puzzle.

My last act in the chapel was to take the ornate water sprinkler from the altar. Superstition, perhaps, but I was dealing with unknown evils! A little holy water seemed like useful protection. Making haste to leave this room, I

found myself back in the great throning hall, and crossed across the yellow W, to the opposite corner of the room.

The Rose Bedchamber

I walked right underneath the legs of one of the giant dragon sculptures to reach the door on the right wall. Behind it, there was a bedchamber with a tiled floor and rose-coloured cloths everywhere, on the table, the bed, and so on. As I approached the fireplace, I noted that the andiron to the left was loosened and went to tighten it, almost absently. Truly, what difference would one tightened fireplace ornament make in this deserted castle? Although this room, too, had that odor of disuse I had noticed in the chapel, the colours were cheery enough that I was not overwhelmed with the loneliness of it all. I went quickly through the little hallway hung with pink curtains, and found myself in another small chamber decorated in that comforting rose colour.

This room had a chest over to one side, which I was unable to open at first try. Turning, I saw the chessboard and went over to it to take a closer look. It was still set up in the middle of a game, by Harssk only knew whom, and how long ago. It appeared that black had the advantage, and at this thought I shuddered uncomfortably. Perhaps this was a metaphor for the state of this castle. . .

As I leaned up from the board, I banged my head on the low-hanging chandelier above the chessboard. Cursing aloud as I steadied myself, and the swinging chandelier, I heard a peculiar rattling sound coming from it and reached inside. I found a cold metal object — a key! It had to be for the chest. Excited, and rubbing my head where a nice knot was forming, I rushed over to the chest to see if the key would fit. Oh, this was a tricky place, with many hidden treasures, I was sure. Silently, I thanked whoever had secured this key in that chandelier, as I inserted it into the chest's lock.

The chest popped open with a squeak, though it was not filled to the brim with treasure, or clues, or anything like. There was, however, a second gold piece, and that was

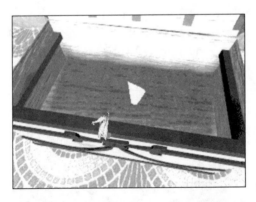

good enough. I took it, and fitted it carefully to the first one. The two pieces blended together flawlessly. The one large piece, formed from the two, had some intricate insignia on it that meant nothing to me. It also appeared incomplete. But I was confident that I would soon unlock this little mystery, and so I put the one large gold piece back among my possessions, and left the chess room through the pink curtains.

The Misty Staircase

As there seemed little to do here, I made my way back to the throne hall, and looked about for the next door to explore. I turned to my right, to enter the door I found, just to the right of the throne, and found myself on a very cold staircase. As I tried to ascend the stairs, I found my passage thwarted by a strange and clearly magical mist. I could not get through this mist, as it gently sent me back to the foot of the stairs each time I tried to pass it.

So, I turned to go down the stairs, instead. There were open windows along the great stone staircase, and the wind was whipping through them in alarmingly cold blasts. I was shivering and rubbing my hands together, all the way down. At the bottom of the stairs, I faced a door which had a shallow indentation on it. This door would not open, no matter what I did. Crestfallen, for I couldn't go up the stairs, and there was nothing to do down here, either, I turned to return once more to the throne room.

The Throne Room (again)

To the left of the staircase, tucked behind the central pillar, was a sword. At first glance, I thought perhaps I had found a better weapon. Upon closer scrutiny,

however, I realized that the sword was more of an ornamental weapon than a useful one, its blade being hopelessly dull. I took it along, anyway. Undoubtedly there was a use for this, somewhere.

In the throne room, I turned abruptly to my right, walked by the throne, but then stopped to face the imposing regal seat. There was an enormous brass serpent upon it which fascinated me, and I went up to it to get a better look. As I reached out to run my fingers along its cold surface, I was momentarily overcome, and sensations flooded over me, coming from I know not where. My vision blurred until all was dark, and then I saw, in front of me, quite distinctly, the faces of men I did not know.

The harsh faced man spoke first, "My master, Haagen von Diakonov, sent me with a gift, Lord. It is a token of the new peace between the Dragon Knight families."

My ears pricked up at the mention of that horrible name. This was no gift of peace, that was sure. I mistrusted his insinuating tones; nor did I like the half-open eyes which darted everywhere, restlessly. I had first seen that same expression as a stripling, on an animal that Brutus had brought down. My adopted father had called it a weasel.

As I was straining to understand this dreamlike scene, the second man, red-haired like me, noble of bearing and warm of voice, spoke. I knew

without a doubt that this was my father, Axel von Wallenrod. Paralyzed, as if trapped in a nightmare from which there is no escape, I listened to his graciousness in the face of treachery.

"A noble gesture from my old enemy," spoke my father. "Thank your master. A serpent of brass! And finely wrought." There was a brief silence, and then my father continued in an agitated voice, "What is this? There is dried blood on this serpent's head!" I felt my heart drop into my toes. I didn't fully understand yet, but I knew that I was witnessing my father's undoing. I could feel it.

The weasel-like man responded in a calmly menacing manner, "Your blood, Lord! You recall that all the Knights gave a phial of blood to each of the others, to seal the Pact of Peace!" His smug manner made me forget that this was but a vision, and as I moved to rip his throat out, all I grabbed was air.

"Treason!" shouted my father, and he groaned from deep within his body. The sound resonated in my heart. I felt the life run out of him, as surely as though it were my own flesh weakening. I began to choke as the proud Axel was dying, all over again, in this terrible vision. "May your bones rot before my throne," he cursed at the agent of Diakonov's treachery. Then, and I swore it to be so, my father turned to face me, looking right into my soul. "Werner!" he cried out hoarsely, "avenge my death!"

And so ended his life. The dark blur of consciousness overcame me once more as the vision ended, and I was left standing before the silent throne, tears streaming down my face. My stomach was so knotted, as the room lurched before my eyes, that I feared I would spill its contents, right here, on the floor of

Treason! Aaagh! May your bones rot before my throne! Aaagh! Werner! Avenge my death!

the great hall. Fiercely wiping the tears away with the back of my hand, I sat down weakly on the stairs before the throne. My head was spinning. I rested it on my knees to avoid seeing the room go around and around.

My father was dead. He hadn't died of old age, or plague, or any reasonably expected causes. Cut down in the prime of his life, was he. Treason! Murder! Diakonov! Oh, Harssk, why had I not killed that black-clad fiend when I had first had the chance? He was the sworn enemy of my father. He was my sworn enemy, as well. How could he have performed such an act of evil as to kill a fellow Dragon Knight in cold blood? And how could the other Dragon Knights have allowed this to happen? Could it be that they hadn't suspected the infamous motives of Diakonov?

My face flushed hot when I recalled his insults, his jeering at me. I would, by all the gods, have vengeance. I would avenge my noble father's life. I would kill Diakonov, rending him limb from limb with my own hands, if that proved necessary. The backs of my hands were wet from wiping away the tears, but now there were angry tears mingled with my grief. "I will avenge thee, father," I swore quietly, and promptly fell asleep, right at the foot of the throne, in my shock and exhaustion.

Some time must have passed while I slept there, curled up on the stairs. When I awoke, my body was stiff, and cold, and sore. I stretched out my limbs as best I could. One of my arms tingled with pins-and-needles; I had used it to pillow my head. A cold anger burned in my stomach, replacing the nausea I had experienced before, when I recalled the vision of my father's death and the treachery of Diakonov. My desire for vengeance was so strong I could taste it, burning in the back of my throat. I had to move, and move quickly. I scrambled to my feet, picked up my shield, and stepped down from the throne without a backward glance. I had much to do. I was discovering that anger could be a renewing force, for suddenly I was driven as I had not been before, and I had boundless energy to expend.

The Small Dining Hall

I stalked over to the door at the throne's left, and went inside the room there. Bright red velvet drapes assaulted my eyes, as I looked around what appeared to be a small dining hall. At the far end of the room, I spied some ornamental shields hanging on the wall. They were decorated with crossed swords. The shield directly in front of me was missing a sword, however, and on impulse, I dug out the ornamental sword I had found near the stairway. As I replaced the ornamental sword, the shield swung aside with a rumbling sound, revealing a small shelf behind. Another golden triangle! As I fit this third piece carefully with the other, larger piece I had previously made, it formed a seal with a coat of arms upon it. Now it was complete. The insignia, I was certain, was the coat of arms of my family, the von Wallenrods! After a cursory glance around the dining hall, I returned to the throne room and turned right to enter yet another arched doorway.

Mustard-Coloured Drapery Rooms

As I entered, I faced a stone wall, which was a trifle disturbing. For a moment I thought I'd happened upon a dead end of sorts, but as I turned to my right, I saw two rooms hung with mustard-coloured drapes. The floor of the far room was strewn with bottles. I decided to explore it, first.

The abundance of huge cobwebs attached to cabinets and ceiling corners indicated that this room had not been used in a long while, either. Broken crockery was on the floor, amid tumbled bottles and a fallen bench. As I looked around, hunting for whatever I could find intact, a half-full bottle on one of the shelves caught my eye. There was something in it that I couldn't retrieve. I tapped the bottle with my mace, and shattered it right on the shelf. Amid the fragments and spilled liquid, there was a marble sphere which was painted to resemble an eyeball. Perplexed, I picked it up and studied it closely. Pocketing it, I looked around the room a bit more, but could find nothing else to interest me.

The second room hung with mustard-coloured drapes was just as sparsely furnished as was the other, and equally as cobwebbed. As I ventured into it, I noticed nothing useful, and turned to leave. A figurine over the bed, hanging on the wall, proved upon closer

examination to be a figure of the great dragon god who was man, Harssk. I pried the figure off of the wall, and added it to my collection of goods. Harssk, patron of dragons and adventurers, would definitely bring me luck in this quest. Inexplicably buoyed by the discovery of the figurine, I began to seek the positive omens in my surroundings, even in the presence of evil. I had the figurine of Harssk with me. I was not in this alone.

The Library

Once more, I crossed the great throne room diagonally, seeking further exploration. My destination was the room to the immediate left of the entry door, through which I had first come into this hall. I passed a number of large dragon sculptures on my left to reach this door. As I opened it, chaos met my eyes. Here was a library, or what had once been used as a library. It was hopelessly disordered. Chairs were strewn this way and that, and volumes of books were scattered all over the floor. There was even a portrait of a woman, bearing a strong resemblance to the Lady Chelhydra, hanging sorrowfully askew. The hopeful notion crossed my mind that perhaps she was my mother. . . only to be abandoned. No doubt my mother had been caught in Diakonov's treacherous web, as well. Both my father and my mother were gone, thanks to Diakonov. This bitter reflection caused my rage to flare up again, and I kicked some of the books around, viciously.

Angrily, I looked up from my contemplation of the books on the floor, and noticed a large dragon figure in the middle of the room. It had a chart of some sort on it, which I was able to read. It appeared to be an explanation of the process of freeing a trapped spirit. Oh, this was truly magic!

The chart spoke of the simplest way to free a caged soul, indicating that one would lay the receptacle in which the victim is trapped, usually a small copy of the victim, before the victim's feet. "Then break it with a symbol of Harssk, the God that is Man and Dragon." Lastly, one was to shake holy water over the broken receptacle. I committed these steps to memory, in a hasty way. Perhaps there would be souls to untrap in this castle. Certainly, anything was possible.

I searched among the volumes in the library, hoping to discover clues or references to Haagen von Diakonov, but it was not to be. I found nothing that would serve my purposes, so I left the library.

Downstairs

Once in the main hall, I proceeded straight across it, all the way to the door opposite me, on the far end. I was going to return to the stairs and try my luck going up or down. After all, Harssk was on my side. It turned out that I still could not go up, so I returned to the downstairs doorway, the one with

the indentation in it, and took a good look at it. The carved gap resembled the seal I had made from the three gold triangles, so I pulled out the crest and placed it into the indentation on the door. Solutions seemed readily available in the Castle von Wallenrod, if one knew where to seek them. The door opened.

Pink and Blue Tapestried Room

The sealed door opened into a room which was notable for two reasons; first because it had a fine, though faded, pink and blue tapestry hanging on the wall, and second because there was a skeleton, skewered by what appeared to be a rather fine rapier, on the ground. I walked quickly by the skeleton, and went into the door beside it. A simple storage room lay just behind it. I ignored the collection of barrels and climbed up the ladder. On the very top shelf, there was a key, but it had been broken into two parts. I took them both. Keys were probably quite valuable in a castle with

so many rooms. I had a choice of two doors by which to exit, but I went out the way I had come — the door to the right of the bottles. I rushed through the pink- and blue-tapestried room, avoiding the skeleton on the floor, and went out through the door just across from me.

Pillared Hall

This door opened into an enormous hallway which was lined with marble pillars. Shallow stairs led down onto another level within the room, which was flanked by doors at either end. I was feeling mightily weighed down by all of the possessions I'd been carrying around, so I

decided to free myself of a number of things I probably wouldn't need anymore. This hall struck me as central enough a location that I would be able to find it easily enough, should I have need of any item I'd left behind, here. Looking around to make sure there was no danger in sight, I dropped all of the weapons I'd collected along the way, except for my mace. I also left various and sundry items, like the faerie cloth, the canteen, the walking staff, and the evil sister's key. I held on to those elements I knew to have import, such as the Dragon Rings, the holy items I'd found in the chapel and vestry, anything else I'd found in the castle thus far, my Spell Book and the flint and sulfur. I found that I could cram a fair number of things into the sack I carried, as well, which helped to make room for other possessions.

The Servants' Quarters

Lighter now, I looked to my left, and saw a doorway directly beneath a huge chandelier. I quickly made my way up the shallow steps and went into it. There, I saw a cell bed, made of wood and chains. It was covered with a pale orange cloth, coarsely woven and rough to the touch. Had I reached the dungeon? Had people really slept on these wooden cots? I lifted up the blanket, but there was nothing under it. I wasn't certain whether this was aggravating or a relief.

The other doorway in this room had a broken door in it, which had apparently come right off of its hinges. The room beyond looked intriguing, so I went to investigate. There was an odor of death and dust in it, no longer an unfamiliar scent to me. On my left, there were two more of these strange wooden beds. One of them was broken. On my right, there was the skeleton of some poor soul, covered by another one of those scratchy woolen blankets. To think that this poor unfortunate's last moments had been spent in such discomfort! My skin itched in sympathy. As I went to pull the cover over its head, the least I could do out of respect for the dead, the skeleton's head swiveled clear around and then faced me once again, only this time it had a marble eyeball in its socket! Gingerly, I took the

eyeball, and stowed it away with the other one I'd found. It was a cold, clammy sphere, and I was all too happy to drop it into my pocket on my way out the door at the foot of the cell bed.

Coat-of-Arms Hallway

I returned to the pillared hallway again, only to turn to my left and enter the next door I came to. On the wall, in this long stone-lined hallway, there were granite-gray carvings of the von Wallenrod coat of arms. I went to the right, and trod the long, brown and tan carpet until I reached another door, and went through.

The Kitchen

The door at the end of the carpet opened into a kitchen, and it seemed to me that every fly that ever had inhabited this castle was probably trapped within this airless room. There was an unappetizing carcass on the block

in the center, apparently the source of all of the insect interest, in addition to the meats hanging down along the wall. I advanced toward the small table in front of me, shooing the flies from my face as I went, until I saw a ladle that looked interesting enough to take. I'd had previous experience with ladles, after all, and figured I might find a use for it.

More Servants' Quarters

I beat a hasty retreat out the door from whence I'd come, and continued along the carpeted hallway until I reached a door on my left. This returned me to the pillared hallway once more. I turned sharply to the left, and entered the first door in the adjacent wall. There were more wooden cots in this simple stone room, though no more moving skeletons greeted me. I finally concluded that I was in the servants' quarters, that these beds had not been intended for prisoners, but rather for those who served the von Wallenrods. I went through the door at the end of the room, and entered a similar room, with a blanket-covered cot on the left. There was an enormous water container next to the uncomfortable bed, with a spigot on it.

I moved to the bed and lifted the ragged orange coverlet. To my surprise, there was a small sphere underneath it. I recognized the marble eyeball at once, and took it. I then turned to my right and went out the door there, back to the center of the pillared hallway. I continued along to my left, until I reached the doorway in the corner.

The Smithy

Upon entering the next room, I was momentarily confused. There were pillars here, similar to those in the hallway, and even the same kind of chandelier! A hasty look around reassured me that this was not some magical kind of illusion, for I was in a forging room. There were elements I vaguely recognized from childhood visits to the smithy: an anvil, a firepit, some huge bellows, and a watering trough. I thought back to the broken key I was carrying, and it occurred to me that I could probably repair it by using this facility. Unfortunately, there was no fuel to be found for the firepit. As I searched the room, desperately trying to recall the various steps of blacksmithing, I found a doorway in the very back.

My assumption that this would lead to some fuel source was an accurate one. The little door opened into a room stocked with piles of wood. I explored a bit in the caged room, to my right. Just to the left of

the broken door, there was a burlap sack full of coal. I carried the coal back in to the smithy, and poured the coal into the firepit. Next came the task of lighting it, and it was truly fortunate that I had carried the flint and sulfur hence, all the way from the farmhouse. I put a small

amount of sulfur on the forge's side. I made a spark by rubbing the pieces of flint together, and held the sparking rocks to the sulfur, thus igniting a small flame. This I quickly transferred to the coal in the firepit

and soon had a faint blaze going. My next action was to pump the bellows at my humble fire, until the coal really caught and was merrily ablaze. When I judged it hot enough, I fished the broken key pieces out of my sack, and held them to the flames. As the key pieces glowed red, I moved them over to the anvil.

Now I needed an implement to pound the key back into one piece. Searching hastily around the room, for I needed to find something before the key pieces cooled too much, I found a hacksaw in the kettle near the anvil. Although this wasn't exactly the kind of tool I needed, I kept it anyway. As I continued to search, I found a table behind the bellows which held many such instruments. I picked up a large hammer and returned to the anvil to

pound the red-hot key. I had never done so before, but I had watched the process many times and so it was not entirely unfamiliar to me. My fear was that I would hit the key wrongly and cause the softened metal to distort. I had no desire to make an unusable key.

Once I had beaten the key so that both pieces were fused together again, I hunted around for my ladle and dipped it in the water trough. I knew that the key was still far too hot to touch, and that my hand would be seared through and through if I even so much as attempted such a thing. As I poured the scoopful of water onto the key, so much steam arose from it that my eyes were quite stung for a moment. The heat was overwhelming. Once it had cleared, though, I saw that I had succeeded. There was a

restored key, in front of me, on the anvil. My curiosity as to its use was
enormous, and I bounded out of the smithy, key in hand, to find a door
which matched it.

As it happened, I didn't have to search far. Down the shallow stairs of
the pillared hall, I found a set of double doors at the end of the lower
level. They wouldn't open until I fitted the newly restored key into one
of the keyholes and turned it. . . .

The Tunnel

The doors opened up into a subterranean tunnel. The floors were
crudely tiled, and the ceiling crudely beamed, but the walls were of
rocky earth. The narrow passageway had a coolness to it, which was
refreshing after the stale, hot air inside the castle rooms I had already
explored. The passage twisted, and I went down a few shallow stairs
until I reached the double wooden doors at the end. These, fortunately,

did not require another key to enter, so I proceeded through them, into yet another imposing hall.

The Three-Headed-dragon Room

This hall was quite unique, for although it had the same marbled ceilings and floors which pervaded the castle, a large portion of the floor was sunken, forming a circular depression. At its center, an enormous, imposing sculpture with three dragon heads seemed to sprout from a stone base. Stone pillars, many times the thickness of the pillars in the hall above, dominated the room. To my right, there were cages along the wall that didn't look too appetizing to me. I didn't intend to investigate them first.

The Armory

I turned to the left, and entered the doorway in the corner. It led into a room filled with weaponry of various sorts, an armory. If I hadn't been so pressed, I should have liked nothing better than to remain here, trying out and testing each weapon. Shelves of swords and maces and all kinds of

weapons lined the roughly hewn stone walls. The large stone tables in the center of the room contained giant glass blocks, each block connected to the ceiling by means of a strong chain. It appeared to me that there were items inside the blocks, but it was difficult to tell exactly

what they were. I tried to lift the glass off of one of them, but the heavy block seemed to be fused to the table upon which it sat. There was no moving it.

Frustrated and bursting with curiosity about the glass blocks, I walked along the wall to my left, until I came to a shelf upon which I found another marble eye, bringing my collection of eyeballs to four.

Not for the first time, I wondered what purpose these eyeballs might serve. I didn't have to look too far for the answer, as it turned out.

Continuing to prowl uneasily around the walls in this dimly lit room, I came across a pillar upon which hung a metal skull, with an iron ring where its jaw should have been. The gaping eye sockets held my attention for a long moment. "I wonder..." I said to no one in particular, as I rolled one of the marble eyeballs around in my hand. Feeling more

than a little foolish, like a child reaching into a jar of sweets, I tentatively stuck the eyeball into the socket of the skull fixture. To my great surprise, it fit perfectly!

As strange noise behind me caused me to jump. I spun around and received quite a shock. One of the glass blocks near me had been removed. I quickly placed an eyeball in the other empty socket,

whirling around to see that yet another of the glass blocks had been removed. In their stead, were a beautiful shield on one table, much more ornate and far better constructed than my own, and a sword of surpassing grace on the other

table. I quickly took them from the tables, and looked around the room for more such sockets. I guessed that the return of the marble eyes had triggered some mechanism to lift the chains above the glass blocks, for the blocks were now hanging, above each table, close to the ceiling.

There was another pillar across the room, similarly equipped with an iron skull. I crossed to it quickly and returned the eyeballs to their sockets. Again, the phenomenon repeated itself. As I turned around to

survey the room, the blocks of glass were gone from the two tables closest to me. This time there was a key to be picked up, and on the

other table, a fabulous crossbow. The weapons were truly those befitting a Dragon Knight, whereas the key . . . well, I wondered where I would find a door to match it. I had no doubt that I would discover it. But when? And where?

As I wandered around the inside of the fountained hall, there were no obvious places for me to use the key I had just discovered. I walked around the circular stairs, to my right, past the cages. I noticed that one of them contained a skeleton, but I couldn't bring myself to get any closer to it. Not for the moment. I had had my fill of skeletons for a while.

The Torture Chamber

I entered the arched doorway, past the cages. The room I entered there flooded my nostrils with an overpowering stench — of rot, and pain, and evil. This was a chamber of torture! Instinctively, I covered my nose with my hand, but there

was no time to defend myself against mere foul odors. There was a wild-eyed man charging at me, with a huge club. His hair was matted and

sticking up straight in some places; he was red-eyed, and bare-chested. I doubted whether he'd ever seen the light of day. I pulled out my mace and stepped up to strike him with it. He shrieked insanely as he struck at me with his club. Around and around the macabre Catherine's wheel I chased him, striking at him as I could, and

fending off his blows. Finally, I was able to deliver a death blow to the mad creature, and he collapsed into a heap on the floor. Filled with loathing and angered by my surroundings, I walked around the room, allowing my sight to be filled with the cursed implements of torture. Some of them still had the skeletons of their victims in them! The stench of rotting flesh emanated from a corner where a corpse was decaying. I tried not to look too closely at all of this death and evidence of torture. How came this room to be in my castle? Who was responsible for this? Had Haagen von Diakonov taken over the Castle von Wallenrod, exerting his power and his evil influence everywhere? The thought only served to fan the flame of my vengeful rage at him. I felt certain that this chamber had not been a part of the castle when my father, Axel, had been the Dragon Knight in residence. No von Wallenrod would allow such pain and suffering!

Horrified by the piles of skulls and the piteous skeletons trapped in the torture devices, I passed a cursory

glance around the chamber, to see if there was anything I could use. On a round table in a corner, there was a pair of tongs. Wincing as I did so, I picked them up and took them with me. I did not like to think that I carried an implement of suffering, and yet I thought perhaps I would have need of them. Possibly, I would redeem the tongs from the taint of their past uses. Once I had them stowed safely away, I left this room in haste, saying a prayer for the souls of those who had been so ill-used here. I offered no prayers for Haagen von Diakonov. He deserved much worse than this. I intended to see that he got it.

The Great Cistern

As I left the torture chamber, the calm air in the dragon sculpture room was refreshing to me. I inhaled deeply, shaking off the horrors I'd just witnessed as I filled my lungs with good, clean air. There was a door directly across the hall from me. I decided to go in and have a look. As I entered the white, marble-walled room, the sound of water dripping greeted me. There was a door in front of me, a sturdily bolted one that would not open. I climbed the marble stairs, and grasped instantly that it was fortunate the door below hadn't opened, for I might have drowned in the contents of the pool I found. The marble pillars all around it served as the only ornaments in the otherwise simple room, though on the wall behind me there were beautiful marble carvings. The sight of the water below was so inviting that I jumped into it without a second thought, clothes and all. I wanted to rid myself of the lingering stench of that torture chamber, as thoroughly as I could.

Once beneath the surface, I swam around and rolled in the water to my heart's content. What a wonder it was, to plunge myself in and feel cleansed of the traces of evil! As I swam, I noticed a gleam in the corner of the pool. There was something on the floor. I went over to it, and found it to be nothing more exciting than a handle of some kind, a mechanical tool. Why was such a thing discarded in this pool? Or was it hidden here? The hair on the back of my neck stood up. I didn't really stop to consider it; I just swam down to the bottom and picked up the crank.

I had come to believe that nothing was just left lying around this castle — everything I had found thus far, especially in the most obscure places, had had use and meaning. It was as if someone had left objects around, or hidden them, so that I would someday find them. I wondered if this was the legacy of my father, in the face of his own suspicions of von Diakonov's machinations. Had Axel known that this day would dawn, when I would return to claim my rightful place without him to guide me? It seemed certain that he did. Or maybe I was creating some other reality, in order to comfort myself. It was, after all, quite lonely in this empty, haunted castle, and I was searching for meaning where, perhaps, there was none to be found.

The most perplexing element of this pool, though, was the fact that it contained two doors — under the water! One, I had already seen from the other side, but the other led . . . I wondered where. It was almost as if this pool wasn't meant to be filled with water. Or perhaps it was sometimes filled and sometimes empty. I swam over to the wall, just to

 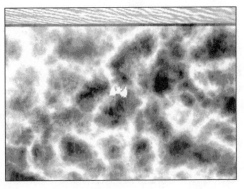

the left of where I'd found the crank, and pulled myself up, out of the water. Dripping wet, I wrung my hair out, and shook off water like a dog. My clothes were plastered to my body, and even though I wrung them out as best I could, I still made a squishing sound as I walked.

The Fountain Room (again)

As I left this room, I paused again to survey the firmly bolted door. Where did that other one, the one inside the pool, go? My curiosity piqued, I decided to find a way to drain this pool so that I could find out. I was still puzzling on this as I walked around the corner, to my right in the sculpture room. There, against the wall where I hadn't seen it before, was a small pool of stagnant water. Above the pool hung a dragon sculpture, much like the ones in the center of the room. This pool seemed to be on the same wall as the larger one was, just behind the wall in the other room. How had the water gotten there?

As I examined the head of this dragon closer, I perceived that there was a gaping hole in it. In a flash, the pieces all came together. This was a fountain! The dragon's head was the spigot, and the water was supplied by the other pool. All that was missing was the handle, the crank, that I could now provide! With a feeling of

excitement fluttering in the pit of my stomach, I fitted the crank to the hole in the dragon sculpture's head and turned. And turned. Oh, Harssk, but it was stiff! A trickle of water came through the mouth of the sculpture. As I persevered, the crank got easier to turn and the trickle suddenly gave way to a veritable flood of water. The sound of rushing water was everywhere, and yet, for all the water that came from the dragon's mouth, the pool beneath it filled, but didn't overflow as I had expected it would.

It was only when I turned around in the hall that I understood why the fountain's pool couldn't overflow. The sunken circular floor in the center of the room was no longer visible, for the three dragon heads were spewing water into what was now an enormous pool of water! They, too, formed a fountain. Enchanted by the fruits of my labor, I stood for a moment and listened to the fountain's merry song of falling water, feeling its spray on my face.

This, I felt, was how the Castle von Wallenrod was supposed to be. Full of fountains and peace, not torture and rot.

Although I wanted to return immediately to the marble pool room and see if my guess had proven accurate — that the pool was gone, leaving that mysterious door accessible — I knew I had one more matter to take care of in this hall. I couldn't deny the skeletons in the caged cells anymore.

The cage farthest to the left contained a skeleton standing against the bars. I wondered what crime this one had been accused of. Whatever it was, I was certain it hadn't been a just sentence. The middle cell contained a small skeleton, too small to be real. It looked like a figurine, and I gingerly picked it up. There was also a sword in this cage, which I ignored entirely. It gave off some foul kind of scent that I mistrusted. When I entered the far right cell, I was instantly struck by the similarity of this skeleton's position, chained up to the wall, to the little skeletal figure I had picked up. In fact, the little one appeared to be a replica of the life-sized one.

It was at this moment that comprehension flooded me. Effigy. Person. Likeness. The soul of this dead person chained to the wall was

trapped in this skeletal effigy, just like the chart in the library had explained! While I struggled to recall the exact order of the steps, I placed the little figure on the skeleton. I took out the effigy of Harssk, and smashed the little skeleton to pieces with it. Then, I placed the holy book upon the skeleton. Finally, I shook some of

the holy water on the skeleton, and touched the skeleton's head briefly. As I did so, its soul must have been freed, for it disappeared completely, along with the holy elements. I turned to leave the cell, my

foot catching on something on the floor. There was another mysterious key! It must have been left behind, released along with the spirit of the skeleton. I picked it up, and went back to the room with the marble pillars and the pool of water. I was going to try that doorway, now.

The Cistern (again)

As I entered the pool room, the sounds of trickling water were fainter than they had been before. I jumped onto the now mostly dry

marble bottom, and ran to the door at the end. To my surprise, it pushed right open, without the need of a key, and I found myself outside the castle, on a planked wooden path.

The Dragon's Lair

I followed the path around to my right, walking around the castle walls. The wind had died down, and there was birdsong in the air. After several paces, I reached a crude archway, resembling a mouse's hole, that had been carved into the castle wall. It opened into a huge cavernous room, with earthen walls and ceiling and floor. In the center of the torchlit hall stood an enormous dragon. I knew at once that this dragon was ally, not foe. There was something incredibly familiar about him, but I couldn't quite determine why I felt this familiarity. I just did.

I approached the dragon and greeted him. "Von Wallenrod!" he boomed in response. "Blood of my blood. Our ancestors fought and died together!"

At this I bowed my head, out of respect for the enormous dragon. He continued, "Your path has not been easy. With no family left, you must conquer your own castle! And I," the dragon confessed sadly, "am a prisoner."

How could such a magnificent, magical beast be a prisoner? I didn't ask the question aloud, yet the dragon responded as though I had. "The foul Diakonov had your father murdered in his own throne room! And I was imprisoned by magic." Now I understood. This marvelous dragon was the dragon of the von Wallenrods, the one which had bonded with us, the one which we rode! And Diakonov's magic was greater still than that of the dragon. He is too powerful, I thought. How could I ever confront him and win? Despite the shiver which ran down my spine, my anger intensified. I felt it begin to burn again in my stomach. I would persevere. And I would be the victor, in any conflict with Haagen von Diakonov.

The dragon spoke again. "My manservant was killed, but his soul was given no rest!" I assured him that I had already dispatched the soul of this man, with sacred honor, and this knowledge seemed to cheer the great wine-coloured creature. Producing a jar, he gave it to me, saying, "I cannot move, but I can help. Take this powder. Use it to reach the first upper level of the castle."

I took the powder gratefully. Perhaps now I would make it up those stairs. "There is a service I would ask you to do for me," the dragon stated, fixing his great orange eyes on me questioningly. I nodded solemnly.

"Bring my son to me," he intoned. "He has waited too many years in the egg; it is time he saw daylight." I was more than delighted to have the chance to perform so significant a task for such a noble dragon as this.

I listened carefully to his instructions as he told me where to find the egg. It needed to hatch in a nest, "which you will find without difficulty," the dragon assured me. It also needed the heat of the Molten Sphere to cause it to hatch. I had an awful feeling that the Molten Sphere was the glowing orange ball I'd seen in the very entrance to the castle, guarded

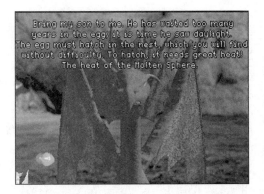

by that gigantic and fiercely protective dragon. The dragon confirmed this suspicion. How would I ever wrest the Sphere from such a beast?

"Here is something to put the guardian dragon to sleep!" And he gave me a small vial, which I presumed contained a kind of sleeping potion. I took it from him, holding it tightly in my hand. The dragon finished, "To give its heat, the Sphere must be broken in the nest." And then I was on my own, armed with a flacon of sleeping powder and a jar of magical dust.

I left the dragon, and went into the doorway in front of him. It looked as if it would lead back into the castle. In fact, it led into an enormous domed hall with dark marble floors and an elaborately carved cabinet on one side. There was an ornate lance on the cabinet, and a beautiful, intricately wrought

saddle. Both were so cunningly constructed that I knew humans had not created them. I took them both, although they were rather heavy to carry. My attempts to open the other door at the end of the hall, however, proved to be in vain. Even the new key, although it seemed to fit the lock, wouldn't

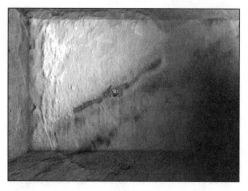

open the door. Not overly daunted, I turned around to go back through the dragon's chamber and outside once more. When I returned to the pool, I crossed to the other door, and turned to the right to pull myself up over the marble edge.

I returned to the hall with the dragon fountains, and was amazed to discover a staircase across the hall from the small dragon fountain, in the corner. As I went down the stairs, I was met by a door which

looked to be the other side of the one which opened into the hall where I'd found the lance and the gorgeous saddle. It, too, refused to open. I tried to use the key on it, and it opened right away. Now that I had a clear passage to this hall and the imprisoned von Wallenrod dragon behind it, I turned to go in search of the dragon's egg.

The Treasure Room

I was about to leave this hall through the huge double doors, when I spied a doorway to the right of the caged cells. It led to a room I had not yet explored, so I went in. There was a torchlit hallway that seemed a trifle ominous. Then again, every room in this castle was somewhat ominous. I bore to my right and soon came into a fabulous room, hung

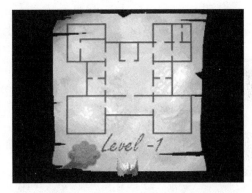

with velvet brocade drapes and stuffed full with gold and other treasures, most of which appeared to be intact.

I had no time for treasure, just then. That might come later, but for now, it was useless to me. There are many kinds of treasure, and a single swallow of water to a man in the desert is worth all the gold in the world. So it was that I found a treasure to meet my needs . . . a map! It lay on the top of a chest, and as I picked it up and thumbed through it, I discovered with delight that it clearly mapped out every floor in the castle. I tossed it in with my other things and left this floor of the castle the way I'd entered, through the wooden double doors and down the earthen passageway. I didn't look back even once at the roomful of treasure.

As I entered the multi-pillared hall again, I saw all of my possessions on the floor as I came through the sunken level. As I didn't need any of them, I turned sharply to my left, and went back through the door in the corner. This took me back into the pink-tapestry room, and I remembered that I had only to make a sharp left, dodging the fallen beams and bits of ceiling blocks on the ground, to reach the door to the staircase.

[Note: Starting on page 195 is a complete set of maps for the von Wallenrod Castle.]

The Guardian Dragon

From here, I returned to the great throning hall, and the door all the way at its end. I went back out across the wooden drawbridge, and paused before the door there, which I knew would lead me to the gargantuan guardian dragon and the Molten Sphere. Taking a deep breath, I prepared myself for the claustrophobic closeness of the room and hoped that I would use the sleeping powder correctly on the dragon. It seemed to me that I would only get one chance. I wanted to break the bottle against the guardian dragon's face, ensuring that some of it got inhaled. "This had better work," I muttered under my breath as I leaned against the door.

The cavernous hall was even more closed-in than I recalled. The dragon was even more gigantic. I knew I had to do this quickly, so I

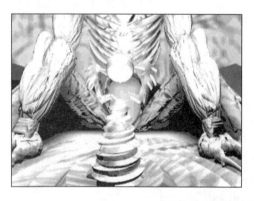 

uncapped the bottle of sleeping powder, carefully pointing it away from myself. Taking careful aim at the head of the mammoth dragon, I hurled the bottle so hard that it smashed into a thousand pieces, right against his jaw. As I watched, the noble beast got a good whiff of it, then became drowsier and drowsier until he slept altogether. The moment his eyes shut, I grabbed the Molten Sphere from its pedestal and shoved it in amid my possessions. Then I ran back through the castle, through the great throne hall. A quick glance at the throne served to remind me of Diakonov's treachery in this very room, and my vow to avenge the death of my father. I didn't stop running until I reached the stairs once more. I didn't have a lot of time to spare.

Up Stairs

Once I stood in front of the strange fog on the staircase, I took out the purple bottle of magic dust the imprisoned dragon had given me. Even the shape of the bottle was magical, I thought as I uncorked it. I threw its contents at the enchanted fog in front of me and the air cleared. I hurried up the stairs until I reached the next level of the castle.

Upstairs Hall and Trellis Room

I found myself in a bright, white-walled hall, with a thick red rug on the floor. I went quickly down to the end of this hallway, and though the set of magnificently carved wooden doors there. They opened into a marble-floored room, which had a staircase on my left and a curiously crafted red trellis on the right. At the foot of the stairs, I saw a green shrub in a pot. There was an odd, tiny metal sphere on the pot which intrigued me; I picked it up and then turned back to face the long hallway once more.

The Nursery

All the way at the end of this room, underneath the mammoth marble staircase, there was a hollowed-out archway, framing a door. My instinct told me to go through it. The door led into a room which made me gasp in a dreamlike recognition. I was in what had evidently been the nursery of the castle, a blue-floored, bright room filled with toys and blocks. A wooden mobile hung from one of the beams on the ceiling. This room was hauntingly familiar to me. The hobby horses, the crib, everything. I had seen it all before, somewhere. Was it a dream? I realized with a start that the crib had been mine —

this room had been mine. Taking a turn around the room, and feeling that inexplicable lump rising again in my throat, I examined every toy, every wooden figure, carefully. When I reached the blocks, I noticed another peculiar metal sphere on the floor among them. It was identical to the one I had just found, so I bent down and picked

it up. This was beginning to feel like a riddle, reminiscent of the marble eyeballs. I straightened up again, and brushed a hand across my eyes. They were stinging and hot.

The Dragon's Nest

I had entered through a plain door; I left the nursery through an ornate one, with a fascinating triangle pattern above it. This opened into a long, sunsplashed hallway, with a gold and dull-orange floor. It appeared that the von Wallenrod coat of arms, by now a familiar sight to me, was inlaid into the shiny floor. I turned to gaze out of the windows. All of that time in the lower levels of the castle had greatly increased my appreciation for the light of day. As I turned to my left, however, I was standing right in front of an arched window covered in thin metal bars. Behind the bars lay the nest of the dragon's egg. There

was another orange and yellow sphere in the nest. Was it another Molten Sphere? I was able to touch it through the bars, though I couldn't pull it out. It did appear to be the remnants of another Molten Sphere, but it was cracked and old.

Fortunately, I still carried the hacksaw I had found in the smithy, and in no time at all I had sawed through the bars and climbed right into the nest with the dragon egg and the broken sphere. An arch in the wall of the nest led to a balcony. I walked out onto the balcony, and took in the view of the window across the way. I took a deep breath of the crisp, fresh air. This, then, was how destiny was created. The simple acts of

restoring cranks and sawing through bars were the cornerstones of its house. I was building my way toward my future as a Dragon Knight, almost without realizing it. I turned to face the egg and the broken sphere. I unwrapped the Molten Sphere carefully and set it in the nest next to the dragon egg. And I waited. And I waited some more. And nothing at all happened.

Finally, I realized that the egg wasn't going to hatch unless I did something to help it along. The Molten Sphere certainly wasn't molten on the outside, yet it was lit from within. The wine-coloured dragon's words came back to me: "Bring me my son . . . the Sphere must be broken in the nest." That was it! The severe heat in the orb could not be released until the orb was broken. Then it would enable the cold dragon egg to hatch. Looking around in my possessions for a suitable tool, I pulled out the torture-room tongs and gently tapped the Sphere with them. This was creating life, using the very instrument of torture and death. As I tapped the Sphere, it broke open and became hotter and hotter until I was sweating profusely. The little nest was so sweltering that I thought the straw in the bottom of the nest would burst into flame any minute. I heard the faint tip-tip-tapping of the baby dragon at the egg. It didn't seem able to break its way out, so I reached over to rotate the egg a bit — and at that exact moment, the baby dragon hatched!

To the Dragon Room

Crimson like his father, with bright orange eyes, the baby dragon stared up at me, innocently. I knew a fiercely protective instinct as I held the little creature, still partly huddled inside his eggshell, and ran through the castle. I hurried through hallways and down stairs, to reach the imprisoned dragon once more. When I reached the fountain room, I was panting and out of breath. The little dragon was beginning to get restless, making little whimpering dragon sounds. I ran down the stairs across from the smaller dragon fountain, and through the great hall where I'd found the lance.

The moment I entered the cave with the papa dragon, the baby ceased to whimper. Its little face grew still and serene, and the enormous dragon was overcome with joy at seeing his son for the first time. He took the little creature from me gently, and cried out, "My son!" As he cradled the baby dragon in his arms, this proud creature turned to me. In his gratitude, he offered to send me to a secret room which was only to be entered by a von Wallenrod.

"If you want to go there," he told me, "you must first give me an object you have touched."

I thought about what I had that I could give him, and handed him an object that I had no use for. It disappeared from my sight forever. "The secret chamber," boomed the dragon, "holds power for you, and also great danger. You must find your own way out!" Certainly, I had not come this far from the humble farm to be deterred by a threat of danger now. I shrugged my shoulders in a gesture of confidence, indicating that I wasn't frightened. And truthfully, I wasn't.

The dragon told me to jump up onto his back and hold tightly, which I did. I could never quite explain the light-headed, dizzy, yet familiar, exhilaration that overcame me and coursed through my body as I sat astride him. The dragon crawled through the tunnel door to the outside,

and we flew though the air, doubling back upon the castle. While we flew, the dragon explained to me that the magic which held him prisoner restricted him to the castle area. He couldn't fly outside of the boundary of the castle's moat. I barely heard his explanation as my senses were overwhelmed by the sensations of riding the dragon of my family. This was my birthright, my heritage! All too soon, he landed near an obscure turret of the castle, one which I had never noticed before, and I climbed off his magnificent back. This was a place which one couldn't access through any other means. The moment I left the warmth of my dragon's form, he flew off, leaving me to fend for myself.

The Teleport Room

I climbed through the fragmented wall and looked around. The room was simple, and white. The ceiling had good strong beams underneath it, and the floor was of that same shiny yellow and orange von Wallenrod coat-of-arms pattern I had seen before. It was dulled in this room, as though the elements had not been kind to any surface, here. Truly, the wind whipped about the small room fiercely, as it was high up in the towers, where the air was turbulent.

I picked my way through the debris on the floor, the fragments of masonry and mortar. The only other contents of this room were a plant

on the wall, a scroll, and a chest. There were no doors, no secret or hidden passageways, no entrance save the hole in the wall I'd come through. I went immediately over to the scroll, which was quite clearly a spell. As I read it, a satisfied grin spread over my face. It was a Teleportation spell! I slipped it into my Spell Book, glancing at it quickly as I did so. Perhaps finding the way out of here would not be so difficult, after all.

I focused my attention on the chest. It contained a number of sealed glass vials — twelve of them, to be exact. With a growing sense of solemnity, I realized that I was standing in front of the collection of Dragon Knight blood, that which had been given by each knight to seal the Pact of Peace. It was an honor and a responsibility to be admitted into this room, I now understood. I thought of each of the Dragon Knights I had thus far encountered. I was standing at the source of their lives. It was a powerful, heady feeling. I counted the twelve bottles over and over again, feverishly. Fujitomo was dead, so it was logical that his blood was no longer here. My father, too, was dead, so there was no von Wallenrod blood in the chest. Diakonov must have broken the wall, and entered this room to get my father's blood! Despite the instant flash of anger that coursed through my veins as I considered this violation and the subsequent treachery it had fueled, my brain was

working coldly, struggling to make sense of what I had seen thus far.

Diakonov had been here, and had stolen the blood of my father, thus severing the Pact of Peace. This much was clear. Diakonov had been here, in this very room. Yet, if twelve Dragon Knights still remained, then his own blood must be among the twelve vials in this chest! Upon saner reflection, this revelation seemed quite obvious to me, and yet at that moment, standing alone in that wind-blasted room, it struck me like a blinding light. Diakonov's blood was here, then, and I was going to find it. He was not the only one who could steal Dragon Knight blood from this place!

On my knees, I searched frantically among the bottles of blood in the chest. Each of them was lettered with faint scratches in the glass. There was a vial marked CL, indicating the blood of Chen Lai, and KvS, that of Klaus von Straupzig. At Hd'A, I paused for a long moment. This was the life blood of Heleynea, the finest Dragon Knight I had ever encountered. I touched the bottle reverently as I replaced it, smiling wryly at the memory of that duel on top of the citadel. Oh, fair Heleynea. I looked forward to our next meeting.

Finally, I came upon what I'd hope to find — the bottle with the faint etchings, HvD. Clenching my hand around its neck, as I would have wished to do to the real Diakonov, I clutched the bottle of Haagen von Diakonov's blood, and straightened up again. In my mind, I visualized the red-carpeted room in the upper levels of the castle, and I cast the Teleport spell, hoping that it would take me there.

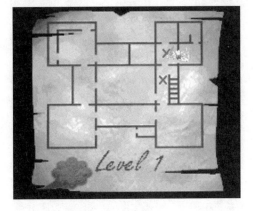

Red-Rugged Room Revisited

So intent was I in concentrating on the red-carpeted room, that I had barely time enough to feel my body hurtling through time and space. In a split second, I came into the red-carpeted room from the air, high above it — or so it seemed to me. The next thing I knew, I was standing in the hallway with the marble floors and the red rug, ready to continue my exploration of the castle. There was a flight of wooden stairs to my right.

Skeleton Room

I decided to see where they would take me. I went through the unobtrusive wooden door at the top of the stairs, and was taken by surprise at the sight of another animated skeleton in the room below me. This one was heavily armored, and I grimly clutched at my mace. The moment he faced

me, even though he appeared to be out of the range of my weapon, I swung my mace and tried to hit at him. I didn't descend the stairs ahead of me, to go down into the room where the skeleton walked. I remained on the landing and kept a height advantage as long as I could sustain it. I aimed for the head of this creature, dodging the blows he leveled at me as best I could.

Blustery Bedchamber

Once the fierce, undead skeleton was dispatched, I cast a quick glance around the simple wooden dining area, and went through the door on my left. It opened into a blustery bedchamber, sparsely furnished, which probably had

been that of some serving women or other upper castle staff. All of the windows were open, and the cold wind whistled through the room. I looked around quickly, and went over to the small cabinet across the way, sandwiched

between two beds. The bottom drawer was open, and I was excited to discover another metal sphere in the drawer. I pocketed it, then turned and went back through the dining area, and up the wooden stairs, returning to the hall with the red rug.

Backtracking

From here, I crossed to the door at the far end of the hall, and went back through the hall with the great marble stairway. I went back through the doorway underneath the stairway, and returned to the sun-splashed hallway via the nursery.

Yellow Bedchamber

This time, I went all the way to the end of the hallway, and passed through the doorway there. It led me into the enormous bedchamber, with the great yellow bed, which must have belonged to my father. The bed was flanked by great metal dragon sculptures, and it came to me with a jolt that this would be my bed, as well. I gazed longingly at it and even went so far as to touch the silken coverlet on the bed. But this was not the time to rest. There was much to be done, and I had a castle to free from evil.

Sunset Room and Bedchamber

I turned quickly to my right and went out the door there, which led into a marble hallway filled with orange sunlight. The walls of this room resembled a sunset, and I thought it the most beautiful I had yet seen in this castle of mine. I went all the way to the end of this hall, and entered another large bedchamber. The ceilings were made of wood carved into

enormous arches, and the floor bore the now-familiar family coat of arms.

The balcony straight ahead of me looked out over the mountains. As I turned to my right, I was startled to be addressed by a little stone creature with orange eyes.

"Master!" it hailed me. "Take me, master! Let me give you the power to wreak revenge on your enemy!" This figure's voice was so insinuating that I was instantly suspicious. The little stone man babbled about wanting to be put into the nest with the dragon's egg, at which point I refused to speak to it at all.

I wanted to have nothing to do with it, so I turned to walk away. Upon entering the bedchamber again, I searched the book-laden shelves until I found a fourth metal sphere. Taking the sphere, I went out the door on the wall opposite the bookshelves, and came into a small space which contained a chair and a table.

There was a curious broken W on the wall ahead of me, and there were three numbers underneath the three plants that were also on the

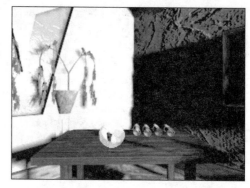

wall. As I advanced to look closer, the scrolls on the table caught my attention. I unfurled the one closest to me. It contained a sketch of a magnificent bird whose wings were aflame. This seemed to be a clue of some sort, but it meant little to me at this moment. I left the scroll on the table, and turned back through the bedchamber, returning to the sunset-splashed hallway again. Once there, I turned to my left.

Royal Council Chamber

I entered the doorway there, and walked into an obviously royal meeting hall. The room was dominated by an enormous mahogany table, and there were chairs scattered around it. I walked around it, and came to a statue of a fine bird, similar to a falcon. Elaborately crafted from real feathers, it rested on top of a wooden stand, adorned with silver mountings. The bird bore a slight resemblance to the bird represented in the scroll that I had just seen,

except that it wasn't on fire, so it was with great anticipation that I examined it more closely. When my examination failed to yield any answers, I looked around the room.

There was a key, hanging high up above the phoenix' head. I could not reach it, though I was

certain it was highly significant. As I went over to the fireplace, I found a small stick in it, which jogged my understanding. Of course! The phoenix sculpture wasn't on fire! But it was supposed to be! I lit the stick with fire made from combining the spark from my flint with some sulfur, and took the small torch over to the statue. As I set the falcon figure ablaze, it gave

off a horrible smell of burned feathers. As I stepped back from it in surprise, I saw that four black holes had opened in the floor at the foot of the wooden stand.

Four black holes. I was by no means dull-witted, but I stood there for a full minute, puzzling it out, before I realized that the four small metal

balls I had collected would fit perfectly into those four holes. I put one of the spheres into the first hole, and the hole covered itself up again. That seemed to be a fairly positive result, so I repeated the process with the other three holes; sticking the balls into them until they, too, were gone. And nothing happened. After waiting for a few moments, I walked up, and touched the falcon statue. I wasn't at all prepared for what next occurred.

The bird burst into flame right under my hand, and spread its wings. As it did so, the stand it rested on opened, revealing a case within, and in the case was a talon attached to some string. I looked at the case, the phoenix, and the talon. There was a key, dangling above the bird's head. As I

examined the key, standing underneath it, I saw that it was hung from an opening in the ceiling. I would find that opening, and use this talon to fish the key up with. This seemed like the sign that the fiery phoenix had given me. I needed that key.

I left the room excitedly, using the door just to the right of the fireplace. As I passed once more through the marbled hallway, I took the stairs going up. There was a door at the top of them which wouldn't open, even as I threw my entire weight against it. I realized that it was locked, and

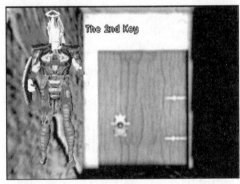

remembered that I still carried the key that I had taken from the table in the armory when the glass had been lifted. I fitted this key to the door, heard the click in the lock as it turned, and sure enough, the heavy wooden door swung open for me with a creak. It opened into a stone room, and directly in front of me was another wooden door, identical to the one through which I had just come, except that this one opened as I leaned on it.

Kettle Room

I found myself in a small stone room. Large black kettles rested on a marble ledge that wrapped all the way around the walls of the room. The windows were open, and the wind was blasting through them. I looked from kettle to kettle, trying to determine if there was anything unique or notable about any of them. I walked about, sniffing them, peering into them, even beating little rhythms on them as though they were drums, but to no avail. They all appeared to be heavy, cast-iron, ordinary cauldrons — save the kettle on my left, the second in from the door.

It made an odd sound when I tapped upon it, a dulled, flat sound, as though it had no resonance. As I peered in it to get a closer look at it, I saw that it had a hole in the bottom! And, as I looked down into the hole, I could see the key, dangling invitingly below, just out of reach. Beneath the key, even farther down, was the tufted head of the falcon sculpture. This reminded me of the talon and string. If I held the string firmly, with the talon end facing down near the key, I reasoned, I might actually be able to fish the key up through this kettle bottom. I was surprised at how easy this turned out to be, though I might have anticipated the result. The talon was, of course, an object of great magic, and, when lowered into the hole in the kettle, it curled itself around the key, holding it firmly in its grip. I reeled the string up slowly, and ultimately had the satisfaction of grasping the key in my own hand. Uncannily, the talon loosened its grip and allowed me to take the key.

As I held it, I turned the key over and over, marveling at its construction. It was made of gold, of this I was reasonably certain, for not only was it intricately formed and filigreed, but it was heavy, too. It was more a work of art than a mere tool, probably intended for a door of great splendour. Clenching the fascinating key in my hand, I left the room with the kettles, unsure of where to go or what to do, next.

Barrel Storage Room

I was near the top of the castle, of this I was certain. The map indicated that there were only two more levels above me, levels resembling those of a turret, and not a whole floor. I stood in the barrel-laden stone room, looking around and wondering where to go, until I perceived the staircase to my right. It was a simple staircase, rough-hewn from some grainy brown stone. The door at the top was locked.

Addlepate's Chambers

Although it seemed highly improbable that such an elaborate key was intended for so simple a door, I placed it into the lock and the door opened almost as if by itself. It opened into what appeared to be a shed, only I was at the top of a castle, so I knew that couldn't be right. The planked room,

though, was indeed constructed similarly to the barn at the farm where Schatzie had spent most of her time. As I turned to my left, however, the room behind the three-pronged archway, belied any resemblance to so humble a building as a farmer's shed.

    The room was lit in an eerie, supernatural light, of oranges and yellows. There was an enormous star pattern in the center of the floor, created from some metal that I did not recognize, though I

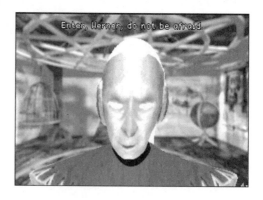

strongly suspected it of having magical properties. From the ceiling, too, hung a similarly sculpted design. Both of them reflected slivers of the golden light which danced all over the room, nearly blinding me as I caught a bright flash of gold right in my eyes. Standing between the elaborate stars was an elderly man, with long white hair and costly robes of black and red velvet, trimmed with gold embroidery. I hesitated. Was this yet another of Diakonv's minions? Another enemy?

The man noticed me, and spoke reassuringly. "Enter, Werner. Do not be afraid." His voice was strong and gentle at the same time, and his eyes were clear and kind. Whoever he was, he was of noble birth.

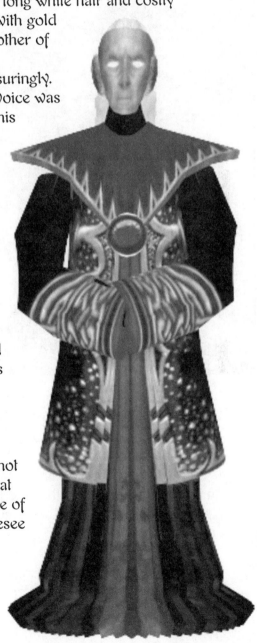

I came forward into his chamber. There were many peculiar things in his room, strange and fantastical charts upon the wall which hurt my eyes to even look at. I did not try to read them. There was an enormous blue sphere in one corner, and an empty bird cage, which looked very old, indeed, in the other.

While I tried to absorb the strangeness of my surroundings, the old man watched me with a half-smile on his face. Finally, he interrupted my curious scrutiny of every corner of the room.

"My name is Addlepate," said he, clearing his throat and looking a bit sheepish. "I served your father, though not well enough. Oh, I knew well enough that Diakonov would attempt murder, in spite of the Pact of Peace . . . But I failed to foresee his method."

My heart leapt at these words, as painful as they were to hear. So I was not the only one who understood the

full picture. Addlepate, too, knew of the treachery of Haagen von Diakonov. Still, I was perplexed. It seemed to me, from his surroundings, that Addlepate was a sorcerer of some kind. Why had he been unable to stop Diakonov?

As though he heard my inner question, Addlepate shook his heard mournfully. "So your father died," he explained in a clear but sad voice, "and I am locked in my chamber. Diakonov's magic is greater than mine, you see."

I had so many questions. I was sure that this old sorcerer knew the answers to them all. Stuttering, I demanded to know why I had been sent away from the castle. Was this more evidence of the treachery of Diakonov? Had it been in order to protect me?

Addlepate smiled. "What you must know is this: like all young von Wallenrod children, you were sent to live among simple folk, as one of them. It is a traditional lesson in humility! As tradition also required," he continued on in spite of my rebellious shrug, "you left the farm on your eighteenth birthday. But instead of being welcomed by your father, you have come to a castle of death!"

Inexorably saddened by this statement, Addlepate seemed nonetheless determined to tell me all that he could. I, too, was saddened by the loss of my father, but I put my grief aside and listened closely.

"Diakonov does not expect you to present yourself for election; he has placed serious obstacles in your path. Even if you do succeed in calling out the Knights, you must win a majority. "

I understood this to be true, and told him so, proudly. I expected to win a majority of knights, without much difficulty. Had not the Lady Chelhydra promised me hers? And Herg the Viking? And Fujitomo?

Again, the sorcerer interrupted me. "You cannot even call an election, if you are not wearing the Dragon Armour, worn by all Knights! Getting the armour won't be easy. You will need to climb to the next floor of this castle and find the way to open your father's tomb."

Of course. It all seemed so incredibly simple and clear. My father's tomb was that of the first Dragon Knight I had ever met, in the Dolmens! But I hadn't known it at the time. The sad irony clutched at my throat, for a moment, making it difficult for me to say anything at all. If only I'd known!

I stalked over to the door, impatient to go. Addlepate's commanding tones brought me back. "But, first, you must take the crossbow, the

shield and the sword from the glass cases in the armory, and place them on the floor in front of me."

As I did so, he uttered words that I cannot now recall over the weapons, though my spine froze at the sound of them. Then, the old sorcerer pleasantly urged me on my way up the turret on his balcony, to seek some vague secret of my father's tomb, saying, "We have talked enough for the moment. It is time to act! Climb the stairs, and beware."

The Castle Tower

Reluctantly, I left my weapons lying there on the floor before Addlepate. I strode through the archway on the opposite side of the room, and went through the door I found on the balcony outside. I took the steps up, and came out onto a square stone parapet. The wind was whipping all around me as I walked about the low walls. The structure in the center had beaten brass bars over each opening I came to. I couldn't easily get inside it.

I walked around the whole thing, shivering with the cold, until I reached a larger opening. I went in, and climbed up the ladder I found there. The bloodcurdling shriek of a hawk diving on its prey greeted me, and practically scared me out of my skin. I was on the top of the castle, in a bleak space lined with small marble pillars, supporting the arches all around. It was so cold up here that my teeth were chattering inside my mouth. The landscape beyond the arches looked desolate, and barren, and empty. I glanced down. The floors were the same roughly hewn planks I had noticed outside Addlepate's chamber. Resigned, I gave a deep sigh. Other than these pillars, the planks of the floor, and the ladder from whence I had come, there was nothing else up here. Perhaps old Addlepate had grown forgetful, in his dotage. Perhaps Diakonov had beaten me here. Perhaps there was nothing to be found at all.

I turned to go back down the ladder, and as I did so, I thought I glimpsed, at the edge of my vision, a momentary red shaft of light gleaming from behind one of the tiny pillars. It was an enormous red gem! A ruby! As if in a dream, the words of the guardian dragon at the Dolmens returned to me: "only one man may touch that ruby — he who places its twin beside it on the tomb." This, then, was that same ruby! Thrilled, I ran back down the ladder, then the stairs, never stopping until I reached Addlepate. Huffing and puffing in an attempt to get my breath back, I showed him the ruby.

"You have it, good!" exclaimed Addlepate. "Now you can find the Dragon Armour!" He paused, and considered me for a moment, before continuing. "I'm going to give you something, a magical map of the region. All you need do is choose where you wish to go." And he handed me a large scroll, whose brightly colored drawings depicted many of the places I had seen along my travels. Delighted, I looked it over, and picked out the mushroom village, and the ferry gate near the river . . . and the Dolmens.

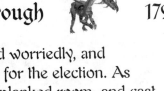
As I took my leave of Addlepate, he fidgeted worriedly, and reminded me to don the armour before calling for the election. As though I could forget it! I stepped out into the planked room, and cast my Teleport spell. Somehow, I didn't think it right to cast my spell in the chambers of Addlepate.

When I had cast my spell, I realized that the map of the land was emblazoned in my head, and I pointed to the Dolmens in my mind — and was instantly taken there!

Back to the Dolmens

As I arrived in the chamber of my father's tomb, I felt a pride and a strength in myself that I had not known before. The same battered green guardian dragon was there, and although we exchanged speaking glances, neither of us said anything aloud. There was no need. I had been to the castle, and I had claimed the ruby which would open my father's crypt. I was Werner von Wallenrod, and I would soon be a Dragon Knight.

In a swift gesture, I replaced the ruby on the side of the casket opposite the other ruby, and a strange red light appeared to glow all around. I crossed around the casket to the other side and went to touch the ruby there. The casket lid flew open,

revealing the skeleton of my father, clad in his armour, clutching his shield. Startled, I found myself hearing my father's voice for the second, and last, time in my life.

"The Dragon Armour of the von Wallenrods! Wear it well, my son. The first Dragon Knight of all

The Dragon Armour of the von Wallenrods! Wear it well, my son. The first Dragon Knight of all was a von Wallenrod, like you! Do not allow the traitor Diakonov to go unpunished for his crime! Justice must be done!

was a von Wallenrod, like you! Do not allow the traitor Diakonov to go unpunished for his crime! Justice must be done!" For a fleeting moment I saw his face before me, the red hair so like my own, and the snapping eyes, and then my father was gone forever.

Though I had become a man, I was not ashamed as I wept, while taking the bright yellow suit of Dragon Armour off of the skeleton of

Fiction Walkthrough 181

my father. I gently eased it off of him, then laid him back to rest in his coffin. I took the shield of beaten silver, which bore the von Wallenrod crest on it, and held it while I surveyed the bare bones that remained of my father.

"Justice will be done." I told them, in a fierce undertone.

I then stood away from the coffin, and closed it for good. Wiggling out of my suit of leather armour, I struggled into the fine yellow and white Dragon Armour. I was prepared, now, to call the election and face Diakonov with the truth of his cowardice.

Return to Addlepate's Room

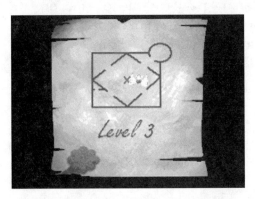

I cast my Teleport spell once more, and returned to the chambers of Addlepate. The old man's eyes lit up as he saw me, clad in the armour of my father — in my armour, now. He was proud of me, that I could see.

"Now, Werner . . ." As he spoke, there was a new confidence in his voice, "Something very important. To be elected by the Brotherhood of Dragon Knights, you must arrive riding on your dragon's back!"

I must have looked surprised, for Addlepate smiled benignly and went on, "As you may know, your dragon is imprisoned in his lair beneath the pool. Unfortunately, I lack the principal ingredient for the spell I must cast to free him."

Was I to go on another quest, then? I was growing impatient to see this one through. At my inquisitive expression, he explained hurriedly, "What I need to set your dragon free is some of Diakonov's blood."

The shock of his words registered deep within my heart. I had
carried that very substance around, pretending to myself that I wasn't
really carrying such a foul burden. . . that is, when I'd even bothered to
think about it at all. I pulled out the vile of gruesome red liquid, the
blood of Diakonov, and held it out wordlessly to Addlepate. "No," he
protested, "don't give it to me. I will tell you how and when to use it!"
He backed away from me.

"Now, we shall capture the enemy in my pentacle!" he told me, an
excited light in his eyes. "Your task will be to keep him there."

Addlepate held out to me a wonderfully cast goblet. "In my chalice,
you'll see an amulet . . . Take a look!"

I peeped inside the chalice. Sure
enough, there was a finely wrought
crimson charm, like a rock but
smooth and intricately carved, on
a piece of silken cord. It looked
very, very old and highly magical.

I looked back up at Addlepate,
and nodded. What did all of this
mean? We were going to kill
Diakonov, weren't we? What was
all this talk of keeping him here?
Despite my confusion, I felt a warmth toward this old man. He was
going to help me to have my revenge!

"When I say 'Leaving so soon?' to Diakonov, you must take the
amulet and throw it at him!" crowed Addlepate, adding, "I would do it
myself, but I'll be busy trying to hold him in place!"

And without so much as an acknowledgment of my readiness or a by-your-leave, the sorcerer summoned an odd light around him, and began to chant. He uttered syllables in that same chilling language he'd used before. This time, it made every hair on my body stand straight up. I wanted to run away.

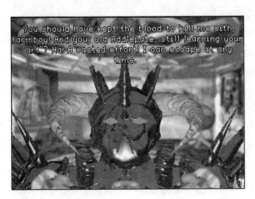

"Thalen ikmal . . . Rescant ikmal. . . . Hirrrk es hirrk . . . Fosnag Thalen! Werner, throw the phial of blood into the pentacle. *Now!*"

I threw the blood into the pentacle, and as the vial smashed against the metallic golden star, Haagen von Diakonov appeared in its place. "You should have kept the blood to kill me with, farmboy!" he jeered. "And you, old Addlepate, still learning your 'art'? Ha! A wasted effort! I can escape at any time."

And he turned in a menacing way, as if to go, or cast a spell, or even attack me, I wasn't exactly sure which. I only knew that I had no fear, anymore.

At that precise moment, Addlepate asked, "Leaving so soon?"

I had my cue. I took careful aim, and threw the charmed necklace at Diakonov. As the red stone hit him, Diakonov's expression changed from one of fear to one of sardonic laughter.

"What!?" he exploded, in bemused but scornful disbelief. "That's your Power Stone, you old fool! The boy's killed you! You'll be dead in minutes!"

What?! What had I done? Yet, Addlepate had instructed me carefully about what he wanted me to do. I had only followed his orders. Had I somehow harmed him? Was Diakonov bluffing? Was Addlepate? Although I didn't understand, a feeling of doom began to grow in the pit of my stomach. The sorcerer shot me a reassuring glance.

"And you will be alive, in my Pentacle," Addlepate responded calmly, "until this castle crumbles into dust! Is that a better fate, Diakonov?"

Diakonov was shocked. "You'd throw away your life, just to trap me here?"

"I may release you," Addlepate told him sternly, then demanded, "You arranged Axel von Wallenrod's death, didn't you?"

"You know I did! He believed I would honour the pact!" Diakonov's arrogance made me want to wring his neck, right then and there. A warning look from Addlepate held me back. I hoped the old magician knew what he was doing.

His arrogance not in the least bit diminished by the fact that he was trapped by Addlepate, Diakonov went on. "You're dying, Addlepate." He seemed to relish the thought as he said it.

"If you are going to release me, it better be soon!" Don't, I begged silently. Don't do it. Make him suffer here, as you have.

"Yes," breathed Addlepate, "I am growing weak. You have an effigy of the von Wallenrod dragon. Drop it!" He began to waver where he stood. I rushed over to the old man, holding his arm to steady him.

Understanding broke over Diakonov's face. "So that's the reason you brought me here!" There was obvious relief in his voice. "Very well . . ." and he dropped a plaster cast of a dragon onto the ground at my feet.

"There," he said nastily, "it won't get the boy elected! He doesn't have enough votes!"

The magician paid no attention to this last, merely intoning his magic spell and releasing the cruel Diakonov from his temporary imprisonment on the pentacle.

Diakonov laughed diabolically. "That's the difference between us, Addlepate! I'd never have released you!"

Addlepate, growing weaker by the minute, smiled weakly at this derision. "Yes," he agreed ironically, "that is the difference between us . . ."

And then Diakonov was gone.

Addlepate turned to me. "Break the effigy, Werner. And take this," he muttered. "You will have your revenge!" He pressed a small, sphere-like object into my hands, and then he slowly vanished before my eyes.

I blinked. I had lost the friend of my father, a great ally. Addlepate had perhaps failed in his duty to my father, but I swore that his actions on my behalf would not be in vain. As far as Diakonov was concerned . . . my jaw tightened. I knew no fear, only a raw, cold anger which would consume us both if I did not triumph over him quickly.

I had no time to lose, no time even to spend mourning the sacrifice of Addlepate's life. That would have to wait until a quieter time. I picked

up the weapons which Addlepate had blessed for me — the shield, the sword, and the crossbow — and then teleported myself down to the lair of the imprisoned dragon, anxious to put an end to Diakonov.

Back to the Dragon's Lair

Once I reached the dragon, I wasted no time making idle conversation with the creature. My dragon, the dragon of the von Wallenrods. I took the figure of the dragon, the effigy, and threw it on the ground. Then I bashed it with my mace until it smashed into a hundred pieces, or more.

Nothing dramatic happened, and for a moment I thought that perhaps Diakonov had devised some other way to keep my dragon imprisoned, but I soon returned to my senses. I went about the serious business of saddling up the dragon, hoisting the huge saddle over his back, above the wings. I climbed up into

the saddle, and without a word, the dragon took flight. It was a serious time, and he knew exactly where to take me. My destination was the Dolmens, and the Seats of Decision. I would delay this election no longer. I was readied for it, strong both in experience and confidence. I had no fear.

The Seats of Decision

We flew up above the castle, high into the air. I savored the feeling of riding my dragon, the dragon of my family. This time, I was at home astride the great beast as its huge wings beat a loud and steady rhythm and we climbed higher and higher into the sky. As we flew over the land, I was able to pick out the places I had traveled through. A strange elation gripped me as we reached the Dolmens. We landed in the midst of the Seats of Decision, and suddenly I was surrounded by the entire group of twelve living Dragon Knights.

The Election

Their expressions were serious, their faces proud. They had come here to vote, and I was here to be evaluated. My day of reckoning was upon me! Diakonov appeared to be in charge. I was angry, but not surprised. No one else knew how diabolical and underhanded he really was! Just wait until they found out!

He stared furiously at me for a moment, as though he could not believe his eyes, then addressed the rest of the knights. "We all know why this farmboy has called us here. I have little time to waste on his farce. Let the voting begin."

Diakonov fixed me with a malevolent glance, then declared loudly, "I, Haagen von Diakonov, vote against!"

Deep inside, I wondered for the first time, why does he hate me so much? He seems to be made of hatred, nothing but hatred.

Then Diakonov went on, in a scornful manner, "The farmboy has somehow acquired Fujitomo's Dragon ring. That is a vote for." I really wished he would quit calling me farmboy, and longed to stuff those words down his evil throat.

He called next upon Arthus of Erwyndell. "How do you vote?" asked Diakonov, arching a sinister eyebrow at Arthus.

Arthus, the knight of green robes and white hair, declared, "For!" I knew a moment of great relief. I already had two votes in my favor, only one against.

The beautiful, though bloodthirsty Tanathya was next, and she looked at me appraisingly before answering, "Against!" in her firm voice. Her response, though, was not altogether surprising to me.

The next knight Diakonov called upon was Herg nach Drakhonen, the Viking. True to his word, Herg voted in my favor. He still had a slightly dazed look on his face, which I attributed to his obsessive fascination with the stone I had delivered to him. I grinned at Herg. He grinned back.

When Chelhydra was called, my ears perked up. Although she had promised me her vote, Herg had led me to believe that I would upset it, in giving him the stone. I was a bit worried, but she dispelled my doubts with her stern, but smiling, "For!" I was profoundly relieved that I had not lost her respect.

The vote got to Sylvan of Sygill and Alexander of Egregalion, the two Dragon Knights inexplicably fused together. Alexander, of course, voted against me. It was only to be expected, after all.

But Sylvan, beaming at me, cast his vote in my favor. "For!" cried he.

I couldn't tell whether he derived more pleasure from voting in my favor, due to the return of his vase, or due to the amount of aggravation it caused

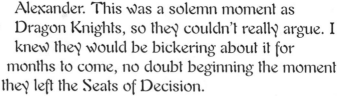

Alexander. This was a solemn moment as Dragon Knights, so they couldn't really argue. I knew they would be bickering about it for months to come, no doubt beginning the moment they left the Seats of Decision.

Diakonov was beginning to look worried. I had already five votes, and needed only one more to be elected Dragon Knight.

He called next on Heleynea, indicating from his tone of voice that he expected such a fierce young warrior to vote against me. Had Diakonov forgotten the ties between her family and mine?

His face fell as the fair Heleynea called out, "For!" and flashed a rare smile at me. That smile warmed me all the way to my toes. I felt my face flushing. I had won six votes. I was now a Dragon Knight, and not all the power of Haagen von Diakonov could change that!

Ignoring this fact, but shaking with rage, Diakonov went on with the process of election. "Chen Lai, how do you vote?" Chen Lai responded, "For!"

I now had seven votes. How many more did I need?

Diakonov called upon the extraordinary cat-man with the striped tail and the hands made of knives. "Klaus von Straupzig, how do you vote?"

Klaus, predictably, voted against me. I hardly cared, even when Kuru, too, cast his vote against me. I was a Dragon Knight already! This was mere formality!

Formar Thain, too, voted in my favor, raising the total of my votes to eight. Haagen von Diakonov looked positively bilious. Had he really doubted me so much? Then he was more foolish than I had thought.

The voting was over. I was a Dragon Knight. Diakonov announced grudgingly, "The result of the voting is for!" I could tell how the words grated and came hard to his throat. Good. How fitting that he should have to be the one to make a formal declaration to my face.

"Werner von Wallenrod is hereby declared Dragon Knight, with all duties and privileges that position entails! Welcome to our Brotherhood, Sir Farmboy!"

My fists clenched at my sides, but I said nothing. I wanted to kill him, all over again. My face flushed, I suppressed the instinct to look down at my feet, and quickly raised my chin even higher and stared right into Diakonov's venomous eyes. My hand on the hilt of my sword bespoke a challenge. The tension amongst us all was thick in the air. No one moved.

Diakonov noticed my gesture, and responded with a jeering smile as Heleynea, unable to contain herself any longer, broke the grim silence by shouting furiously, "Are you going to let him mock you, Werner?"

The result of the voting is for! Werner von Wallenrod is hereby declared Dragon Knight, with all duties and privileges that position entails! Welcome to our BrotherHood, Sir Farmboy!

I was about to draw my sword, when Heleynea turned on Diakonov.

"Treachery, Diakonov!" she cried, her arm extended, its finger pointing accusingly at his face. He took several steps back from her, until his back was against one of the stone seats, and he could go no further.

"The punishment for breaking the Pact is without appeal!" she intoned. "You are hereby banished! Your titles and lands go to Werner von Wallenrod. That is the law of the Dragon Knights!"

Oh, but I was proud of the fierce Heleynea! What a wonderful girl! Diakonov, finally exposed and subjected to the judgment of his fellow knights, had no alternative but to go. Furious but resigned, he left on his dark dragon, and no one could tell where he went. He looked back once — straight at me. I imagined I heard his voice in my head, swearing vengeance. But I did not care. I had other things to do.

Surrounded by the Dragon Knights, who'd suddenly broken their silences and become a joyful lot, I allowed myself to be congratulated by those who had voted in my favor, and even by those who hadn't.

As I left on my dragon, traveling over my lands on the way to the Castle von Wallenrod, I saw again the triumphant faces of Chelhydra, Chen Lai, Arthus, and Formar, in my mind. I relived the dizzying experience of Heleynea's embrace. I was seated upon the back of the dragon who'd been linked to my family. I was looking forward to setting my castle and my lands in order. No longer was I an awkward farmboy, set loose in a strange and forbidding world. I was a Dragon Knight!

But, more importantly, I had grown through the pain and joy of my experiences. I had learned to trust in the value of my own judgment, and to rely on the help of others where I could not succeed alone. I had traveled the land over, hobnobbed with pixies and battled with goblins, casting spells and meeting my destiny. The good Addlepate had given his life for me, and I had lost my father before I'd ever known him. I would never be able to change the fact of his death. Yet, I was his son, and I would carry his name. I had a bright future before me. I was a man!

THE END . . .
FOR NOW.

The Maps

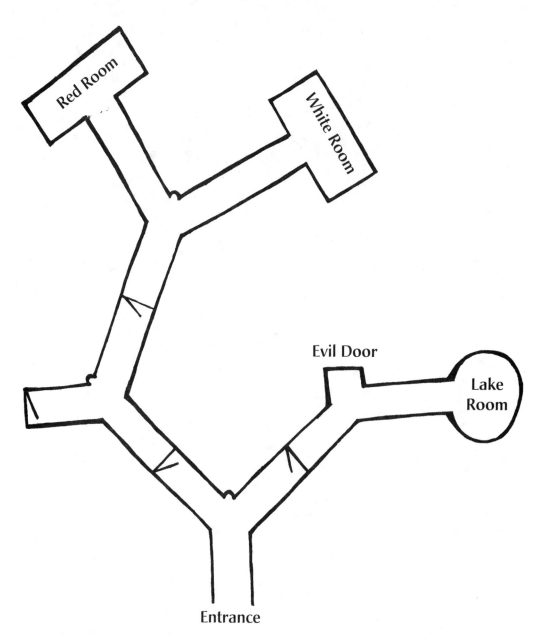

The Labyrinth

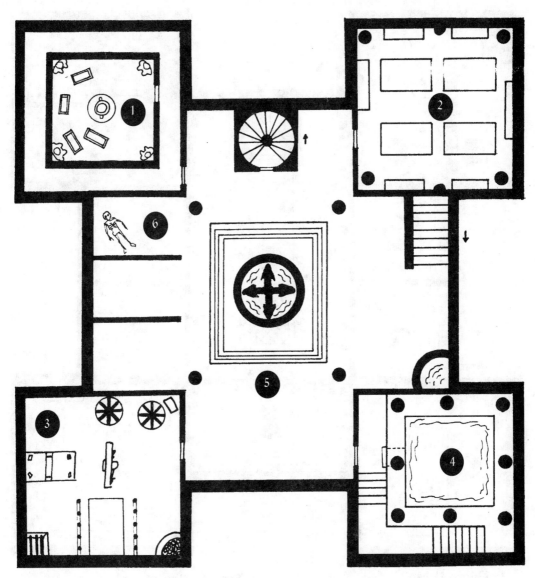

The Castle

Basement Level 2

1. Treasure Room
2. Armory
3. Torture Chamber
4. Pool Room
5. Dragon's Head Hall
6. Trapped Soul

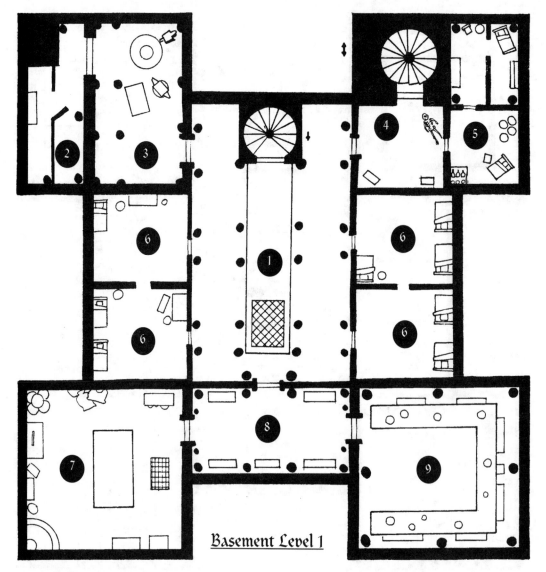

Basement Level 1

1. Pillared Hall

2. Coal Room

3. Forge

4. Pink and Blue Tapestry

5. Ladder Room (Broken Key)

6. Cell Beds (eyeballs)

7. Kitchen

8. Coat of Arms Hallway

9. Dining Hall

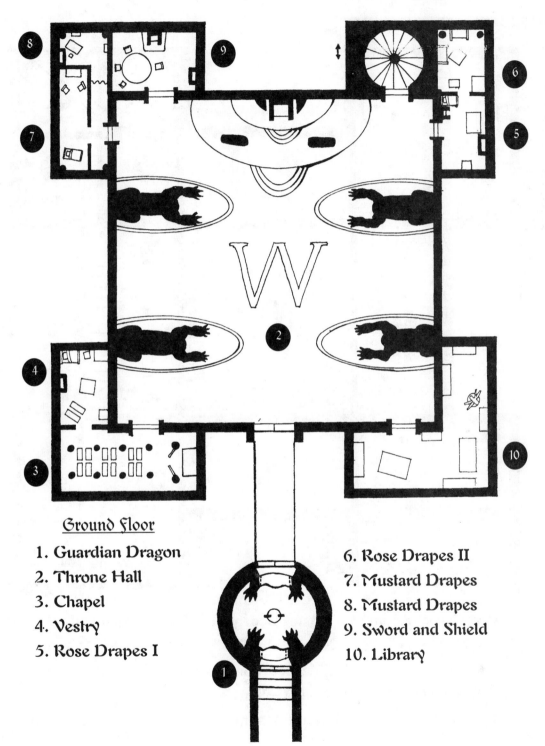

Ground Floor

1. Guardian Dragon
2. Throne Hall
3. Chapel
4. Vestry
5. Rose Drapes I

6. Rose Drapes II
7. Mustard Drapes
8. Mustard Drapes
9. Sword and Shield
10. Library

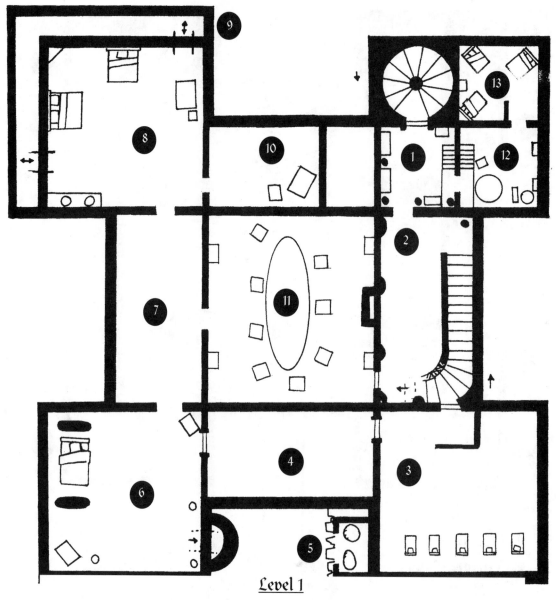

Level 1

1. Red Carpet Room
2. Marble Hall
3. Nursery
4. Yellow Hall
5. Egg Nest
6. Master Bedroom
7. Sunset Hall
8. Side Bedroom
9. Stone Golem
10. Scroll Room
11. Council Hall
12. Skeleton Room
13. Metal Ball

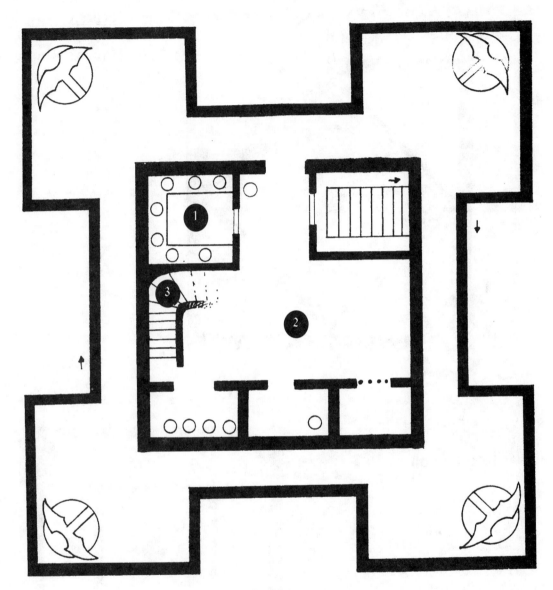

Level 2

1. Kettle Room
2. Barrel Hall
3. Stairs to Addelpate

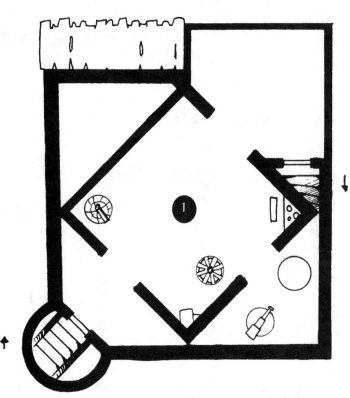

Level 3

1. Addelpate's Room

Level 4

1. Ruby Loft

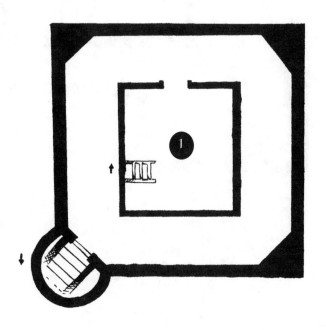

Simple Walkthrough

Simple Walkthrough

THE FARM

Poor Werner, clumsy oaf. Maybe the farming life isn't exactly what you were cut out for. Oh, well. As you turn to the right, the sound of knives being sharpened against one another tells you that you're not alone. No, there's the farmer, your rather gruff adopted father. Talk to him and discover that the cow needs milking, but the pail for the milk is leaking and he needs you to

205

find a bowl or something to replace the leaky pail. If you talk to him too much, he'll get downright nasty. The best thing to do is to go in search of the requested bowl.

Dogs and Cows

Look For: The Bone, the Bowl and the Bovine (and the Rope)

Turn to the right, and go out of the gate at the end of the path. Take the path to the right, pass the panting dog in the pen, to the end of the path as it ends in the far pasture. Once you're in the pasture, head for the small shed. You'll want to pick up the bone on the ground in the shed. You'll be feeding it to that nice but snarling doggie, so that you can occupy her while you're looking for the bowl in the barn she guards.

Out of the meadow, return to the pooch. Knick knack paddy whack . . . take the bone and return to the dog. Left click on the dog (with the bone as the cursor). As you give the dog the bone, she'll walk off with it, into

the barn. Follow her, and you'll see the little brown bowl on the ground to the right. Take the bowl and put it in your inventory.

Take the bowl back to the farmer.

Note: We'll tell you once, and once only. When you're giving something to somebody in this game, be sure to click the left mouse button, not the right. If you accidentally click on the right button, Werner will throw the object he's carrying and if you hit one of the characters in this game with an object, they become downright hostile!

Once you've given the bowl to the farmer, he'll testily ask you to go and tie the cow up in the pasture. Maybe he wasn't cut out for farming, either. Follow him into the house and look around for the rope, which is hanging on a post to the right of the door. Leave the house, pass through the gate again, and take the path off to the left this time.

The cow is off to the right, in the first pasture you come to — the one with the broken gate. Click the rope onto the cow, and she'll follow you, which means, practically speaking, that there's now a large cow icon on the bottom left of your

screen. It'll follow you around wherever you go. Keep that rope in your inventory, though, 'cause you'll need it when you reach the pasture. Lead the cow out through the gate and to the left, back past the house. She has to be tied up in the pasture where you found the shed and the bone. Pay no attention to the panting dog. As you enter the pasture, Daisy will wander obediently over to a tree next to the shed. Return to your inventory, and after choosing the rope, click on her with the rope, and lo! She's tied to the tree. Won't the farmer be pleased!

Conversation with the Farmer

Look For: Ring and Whistle

Head back to the farmhouse and talk to your dear old adopted dad. He's got a mouthful to say to you, so listen up. Guess what? You're really not cut out for farming, after all! He gives you a ring and a whistle. He seems to know a lot about your history, but won't tell you anything other than to head for the Castle von Wallenrod.

Gathering Supplies

Look For: Flint and Sulfur, Armor, Shield and War Hammer

Keep him talking until he tells you to take whatever you need from the farmhouse; you'll need resources as you seek your fortunes. Since he's

given you permission, go ahead and grab the yellow bag from the table. (You can access your inventory by right-clicking the mouse in the upper left corner of the screen.) The bag has sulfur in it, which will come in mighty handy down the road. That shield hanging on the wall will also serve you well in your travels; take it down and put it on your left arm (as you face Werner, in the inventory). The armor in the corner above the barrel fits perfectly. The rock on the barrel is a flint; take it as well. The a canteen on the bed next to the old man, is an optional item. Carry it if you must.

As you head outside, go around the house and pick up the war hammer that's lying on the ground behind the place. Next, come around to the front of the house and look in the cart to the right of the gate; there's an old, bent-up sword in it for the taking.

The Second Dog

Now's the time to run free into the world to chase your destiny, so head out the gate for the last time. You'll want to go off to the left, past where the cow was, and confront another dog. This one's even more aggressive than the last one. He stands right in the middle of the path and will not let you pass. You'll need to go into your inventory, choose the whistle and take it over to Werner's face. This action signifies that he's blown the whistle, and the dog will respond by moving over to let you continue along your path to adventure.

THE DOLMENS

You'll be led down the stone road in an animated sequence, and Werner walks around the huge stone in the middle of the circular road. Follow the white brick road until you come to another obelisk-like rock in the middle of a circular path, and move to the right, around the obelisk. You'll want to head to the left of the two skulls.

Chen Lai

Go ahead and talk to Chen Lai if you wish; you can talk to him now or later — it doesn't matter. Chen Lai's the Dragon Knight who's wandering around on the path. Chen lets you know that you'll need the votes of at least six Dragon Knights in order to become one of them. He outlines your choices: pursuing a path of Force or a path of Wisdom. He votes for Wisdom. If

I am Chen Lai... Dragon Knight. Twelve Knights will vote, and you will become a Dragon Knight only if at least half our number decide in your favour!

Will you choose the path of Power or that of Wisdom? Of Force or Mercy? Or will you take the narrow road that divides the two?

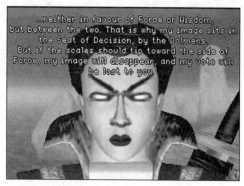

you keep talking at him, he'll let you know how you've been judged thus far in your actions. At this point (assuming you've followed this walkthrough accurately) you've followed the path of Wisdom, which is why his image sits in the Seat of Decision by the Dolmens.

Entering the Dolmens

Look For: Gate Key 1, Button on the Wall

Now your choices are to continue along the path, under the archways, or to turn back and go to the obelisk rock. It's essential that you return to the rock, bear to the left, and go down the path that runs between the two skulls. As you reach the middle of the path, veer left onto the grass. Follow the rocks that have been placed in a circle until you reach the open maw of the left skull. Go on into the opening.

There's a key on the floor in the very back of the hall. Pick it up, and exit this skull the way you came in. Take a left outside the opening, and cross over the path to reach the right skull. Enter the opening to the right

skull. Use the key from the left skull to open the gate (by choosing it from your inventory and left-clicking the key on the gate). Turn right and go down the hallway. Watch out for the skeleton — it's armed and dangerous. Proceed up the hallway by three clicks and push the button on the wall on the right.

The Boulder

That boulder coming at you is more or less harmless — and anyway, there's nothing you can do about it, since it's a canned animation sequence. If you're observant, you'll notice something stuck to the rock.

The Skeleton

You might have to kill that pesky skeleton, if you've not done so already. The war hammer is the suggested implement of destruction. The sword is next to useless as it will break almost immediately. You can throw it at the skeleton, and then use the hammer, though.

To kill the skeleton, start swinging when he's still some distance away. When he's about halfway down the hall, you can hit him. Once he starts to close in on you, run past (actually, through) him as far as you can go down the hallway, turn around and try to get in a few more hits on him. Don't let him get too close — if he hits you three times or so, you'll be toasted in the fires of hell. You should be able to destroy this walking pile of bones without getting hit at all, though. It just takes patience.

Combat in Dragon Lore:

The basic strategy to succeed in Dragon Lore combat is to hit your opponent (whether man or creature) without taking any damage yourself. One highly effective way to do this is to ensure that you have plenty of maneuvering room when you fight. In the case of the skeleton, running from one end of the hallway to the other and swinging at him when he chases you is the surest way to defeat him without taking damage yourself. Don't worry if you don't hit him every time, though. You will get good hits in on him some of the time, whereas he won't hit you at all.

Also, try different types of strokes by placing the cursor at different locations on the screen when you click the button to swing your weapon. Often, a good lateral slash is the best attack. Sometimes an overhead smash works, too. Experiment. And remember to save your game before attacking any creature!

You don't have to kill the skeleton, but if you do, make sure to check his inventory by clicking on his corpse with the right mouse button. You'll get his halberd if you do this.

Getting the Second Key

Look For: Gate Key 2

Step back into the hallway the boulder just rumbled through, and turn right. At the end of the hallway, where the boulder crashed, you'll find a key nestled in among the fragments of boulder wreckage. Pick it up. Then go back down to the other end of the hallway opposite the boulder pieces, and use the key to get through the gate on your right.

Opening the Dolmens Door

Once through the gate, you'll see a trap door in the floor in front of you. Click on it, and Werner will jump down through it into a torchlit room. Go straight up to the big wooden double doors and use your magic ring to get through them.

Inside the Casket Room

Look For: Open Door Spell

You're in a huge domed hall with three chairs directly in front of you. There's a casket just behind the chairs, and a green dragon walking around. Clicking the ring onto the casket, between the middle chair's back and seat, will cause the dragon to speak to you. He tells you that you can touch the ruby on the casket only by replacing its mate in a space opposite it. The ruby you seek is in the Castle von Wallenrod. Well, fancy that. Keep left-clicking on the dragon with the ring so that he keeps talking. He tells you that the ring you wear must be brought to life — it must be forged by fire.

If you are armed at this point, you can kill the dragon. You don't need to do so. It's your choice, but if you do kill the dragon, make sure to check his inventory by clicking on his corpse with the right mouse button. (This will be true of any enemies you kill.)

The dragon will give you a scroll, and as you include it in your inventory, you hold it over Werner's face to find out that it is an Open Door spell.

Exit the casket room and go back up the stairs to the trap door. When you reach the wall, click the cursor up at the top of the screen and watch as the clever Werner crawls up the trap door. Exit the way you came in.

The Seats of Judgment

Once outside, go up the path between the skulls and look at the figures in front of the seats. Chen Lai is there, with a few other Dragon Knights. When you're finished communing with the Dragon Knight figures, turn back to go down the path and go to the right at the obelisk.

Leaving the Dolmens

Go down the path to the right, and talk to Chen Lai again. If you killed the green dragon in the hall to get the scroll, Chen will inform

you that the balance of judgment has shifted to somewhere between Force and Wisdom. He warns you that if your actions veer more toward Force than Wisdom, you'll lose his vote. Turn to the right after talking to Chen Lai, and head down the path arched by rocks. The animation sequence will show Werner walking down the path, as the game takes over for a few seconds. You hear an owl as you stand underneath the rock archway.

The Tunnel

Look For: Spell Book & Using Open Door Spell

Go forward, heading for the mountains, until you reach the wooden door in the mountain. It will open for you, and you'll be in a tunnel underneath the mountain. Ahead of you, there's yet another wooden door, flanked by two torches on the walls. Why won't it open?

Turn around and face the wall. There's a strange spot on the wall which looks a little different from the rest of the tunnel walls. The dragon cursor icon displays some interest in that spot, telling you there's an action you can take here. As you choose the hammer from your inventory and click on this place with the hammer, a little ledge is revealed behind the wall. The Spell Book is on the ledge; take it and add it to your inventory.

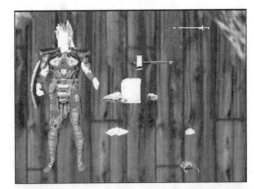

In the inventory screen, put the book down and drag the Open Door spell into the Spell Book. Next, take the Spell Book and put it over Werner's face to read the spell. Memorize the order of the symbols or write them down if necessary. The right mouse button gets you out of the book; your next step is to place the book in Werner's hand to cast the spell. Make sure you're facing the appropriate door before casting the spell. Also, make sure that you're close to the door, as this spell seems to have a limited range.

You'll see the symbols at the bottom left of your screen. Click on the first symbol. It will be duplicated at the top left of the screen. Then choose the next one from the bottom, and so on until all three spell symbols are in order at the top of the screen. Click the right mouse button, and you've cast your Open Door Spell. And, yes, it opens the door leading out of the cave.

The Crossroads

Once through the door, take the Spell Book out of Werner's hand. You'll probably want to save your game here. You'll see some more rock archways to go through. And you'll hear a lot of mosquitoes buzzing around. The game takes over and you'll walk along until you reach a place where the cobblestone path you're on intersects another one.

Just ahead of you is a series of rock arches, blocked by a giant spider web. Turn left and go ahead into the tavern. If you want to follow the path of Wisdom, you'll stick your weapons into your inventory and leave them there while you're in the tavern.

The Tavern & the Dragonfly

Look For: Ladle, Resin, Mace, Fireball Spell

It's a simple tavern, with a few tables and chairs scattered around. Your hosts, George and Albert, are standing behind the bar, and although they're half-witted, they're just chock-full of conversational riches for you. George is the big guy with the

earring. Keep them talking until Albert says you have to pay them a toll, in the form of a few coins. Problem here is, you've got no money. Their solution is to ask you to earn your toll by helping them

out in their nectar-making business. They make the nectar out of resin from the dragonfly hive, and your job is to go and collect some resin for them. They give you a ladle to scoop the resin up with, warning you not to touch the dangerous substance.

After you leave the tavern, you'll go to the end of the path you're on and find the dragonfly cave. Arm yourself with the hammer, and be prepared to kill this thing with three or four good solid hits. The hammer is a pretty effective weapon, so keep swinging and the dragonfly will go down. It has nothing of value in its inventory.

Go forward into the cave, and put the hammer back in your inventory. As you click on the ladle, hit the right mouse button to exit the inventory and carry the ladle. Face the alcove at the rear of the cave. Left click on

the resin pot's base with the ladle and it will be full of the resin. (The ladle will look a little different, but you can double-check that the ladle's filled by holding it over Werner's face in the inventory.)

Carry the resin back to George and Albert, and they'll be happy as clams, not to mention guilty as rats that they've sent you on such a dangerous mission. To assuage

their guilt, they make you a present of a fine Morning Star (a mace), a Fireball Spell, and some rope. Once they've given you these gifts, they won't talk to you anymore, although you can stand there and be entertained for a while if you wish, watching them both beat George's head like a drum. Folks sure are strange in these parts.

The Spider Web

This time, as you leave the tavern, you'll take the path to your immediate left, the one with the space between the arches covered by the enormous spider web. Clue: the Fire ball spell opens the spider web. (Just remember to put the book over Werner's eyes in the inventory to memorize the spell before you cast it. Clicking on the bottom of the screen will turn the pages of your Spell Book, so that you can read the different spells in it. A click on the right button takes the book off of Werner's eyes, so you can put it back in his hand.) Cast the spell, and incinerate the web.

The Ferry Dock (Diakonov & His Monster)

Look For: Oar

Because you're entering into the dangerous unknown, arm yourself with the mace and save the game before proceeding any further . . . then pass

under the rock arches, and prepare for your arrival at the Ferry Gatehouse, where you'll come face-to-face with that fiend, Haagen von Diakonov.

Von Diakonov is the violent, bloodthirsty sort who won't talk to you at all until you attack him. As you go to hit him with the mace, he'll taunt you about your inability to find the barge-pole. Clearly he has no love for you, as well as a wicked accent. He disappears and leaves you to fight his green minion.

You'll want to kill this miscreant as quickly as possible. If you can move away from it the moment you see it, you'll help yourself out a lot. Attack it with the mace as it approaches you; a few good hits will wipe it out. The secret is to keep moving around, so that it has a hard time hitting you. Check its inventory and you'll pick up its cleaver, as well

as the oar for the ferry. The cleaver has seen better days, but the oar is a necessity.

Continue straight through the building and onto the ferry. As you click the oar onto the pole on the bottom right corner of the ferry (look for the dragon icon to show interest in the spot) and then step onto the wooden surface, the boat will take off and you'll cross the river.

Fomar Thain

Once on the other side of the river, you'll see huge rounded stone arches and a curious blue man walking around them. Disarm yourself if you are armed, and chat with Fomar Thain. He's a nice old man with white hair and pointy blue ears who urges you to maintain the balance of your actions toward Wisdom, not Force. Go ahead and walk forward, until you see the stone pillars and hear the flies. Where there are flies, there must be — eek! Flytraps.

I am Formar Thain of Hav'shal. We shall meet again when the voting begins.

The Giant Man-Eating Flytrap

Look For: Skull (Grappling Hook)

As you turn around, you'll see a huge red plant in the middle of the stone pieces. Do not get near it! Instead, pick up the skull just to its right, on the ground. Don't walk forward, just click on the skull from where you're standing. Go into the inventory, click the skull on your rope, and you now have a grappling

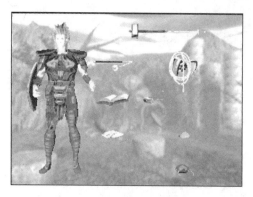

hook. Click it on the branch to the left of the Venus Flytrap and watch as Werner goes right over the nasty hungry plant. Put away the grappling hook and talk to that impatient-looking woman behind the tree.

Tanathya

Tanathya is one of the more bloodthirsty of the Dragon Knights, but she's civil enough to warn you about the difficulty involved in getting into the castle. She tells you of Fujitomo, a dead Dragon Knight whose ring has never been claimed. Yet. Tanathya explains that if you get the ring of Fujitomo, you will automatically have that vote for

yourself. Furthering the cause of bloodshed and violence, Tanathya also makes it clear that her loyalties rest with a man whose blade runs red with blood. Nice girl, even though she does have strange taste in plants. Go ahead and pass around behind her, down the path. (Don't go off to the left, unless you're prepared to face her wicked man-eating pet and do the grappling hook maneuver again.)

The Mushroom Village 1

The path takes you across a little stream. At the end of the wooden bridge, you'll face some giant toadstools. The strange blue lady is Chelhydra, and she teases you about your size. Unless you're smaller, you can't visit the sprites in the toadstools, which is something she seems to want you to do. Chelhydra is another Dragon Knight and her vote will stay with you, if your actions lean toward Wisdom. She's got some sort of rivalry with Tanathya and won't vote for you if Tanathya does.

The Fountain Crossroads 1

As you go around the toadstools to the left, you'll find a bridge leading over the little stream. Follow it, and you'll come to a fountain. Walk around the fountain to the right, and take the first path you come to, the one that's overgrown with weeping willow branches.

The Bad Faerie

Look For: Apple, Faerie's Pet, Lever, Evil Key

You'll be in an icy sort of landscape. In the distance is a kind of treehouse. Under the treehouse, on the path, there's an apple. Go ahead

and pick it up. To the right of the apple a bizarre-looking animal stands, panting; it doesn't seem to have your best interests at heart. You may feed the apple to the creature to keep it occupied, or just go ahead and kill it, depending on whether you preferred Tanathya to Chelhydra. Just behind the place where the happy creature was standing, there's a lever in the ground to the right of the treehouse. Click on it to fly on up to the house. . . .

In the treehouse, there's a pillar in the center with an old faerie lady in it who'll chide you for not having hit her horrible cat-creature (assuming that you fed it instead). She's obviously not too kind a being, and her desire to give you the power to kill only reinforces this impression. The winged biddy gives you a key for a tunnel door. Are you sure you want to use it? As you leave her friendly little treehouse, you'll see a lever on the right. Click on it to leave this sour, white-haired faerie. Back on the frozen tundra, head to the left and between the dark craggy mountains to return to the fountain.

The Fountain Crossroads 2

Once you've come across the fountain again, head straight across, ignoring the path on your right. The path you want has a less

overgrown version of the weeping willow across it. There's a castle-like wooden house with arched windows. Cross over the stone bridge to reach its front door.

The Good Faerie

Look For: Cog, Piece of Cloth

Go into the house and talk to the blonde faerie woman. She's a lot more pleasant than her white-haired sister, and she gives you a cog to put into some undefined place. Next, you'll want to find the staircase and go upstairs in her little castle-house. There's a bureau across from her bed. The cursor

will indicate there's something to
find in the bottom drawer by
showing you an enlarged version of
the pink dragon's eye, and as you
click on the bottom drawer you'll
find a piece of cloth, which you must
take. Head back down the stairs and
then turn around 180 degrees,
because the exit door is in the same
archway as the stairs; just to the left
instead of to the right.

Fountain Crossroads 3

Look For: Water to Wet Cloth

Head back over the bridge to the fountain. Once at the fountain, take the
piece of cloth from your inventory and click it on a part of the fountain
where there's water. The cloth will become a brighter shade of blue. This
wets the cloth so that Werner can use it on his face, in the inventory. Go

to the inventory and click the wet cloth over his face to make a protective mask for Werner.

The Faerie Garden

Look For: Yellow Flowers, Blue Flowers

Now swing around to the left and take the first path on your left, the one which goes between two little rock formations. This path leads to a faerie garden, where there are many beautiful flowers (and a lot of mosquitoes, from the sound of it). As you move forward in the garden, you'll see the pink dragon icon telling you to pick some of the mustard-yellow,

bamboo-like flowers. Pick up two of them. As you turn to your left, the icon will tell you to pick some of the red flowers, but ignore this as they will only cause you harm. The blue flowers, on the other hand, are something you want — go ahead and pick one bunch of them, and no more. Then head back the way you came, returning to the fountain.

The Mushroom Village 2

The path straight across, the one leading between two light-brown rock formations, will take you back to the mushroom village. You'll see the blue Chelhydra wandering around, but she's more interested in how you fare with the toadstool sprites than in conversation, and she won't talk to you anymore.

The Blue Flowers and the Red Scorpion

Look For: Blue Bottle

Now that you're in the mushroom village, you'll need to move closer in among the toadstool houses. Walk past Chelhydra to do so. Do not attempt to shrink before you have armed yourself with the mace (and possibly saved your game). Shrink down to sprite size by choosing the blue flower from your inventory and placing it on Werner's face.

Now go looking for a giant red scorpion before it finds you. Hopefully you've moved far enough into the toadstools that you can see it coming from a distance. Strike at it as soon as you can. Don't stop to ask questions, just kill it. It's got a mean sting and it's best to try to hit it when it faces you, a little way off, using a slashing attack. Don't let it get too close!

One secret to killing the scorpion is to find the blue-gray bottle on the ground, and then head to the right of it, through the village. A clearing just beyond the mushroom village leads to the creek. From here you can maneuver around, dodging the scorpion when it gets too close. Otherwise, it'll back you into a corner quickly and make toast out of you. The idea is to click really quickly to get past it, then turn around and get a few good hits on it until it's too close, then repeat. Aiming slightly off to either side of the scorpion results in a great sideswipe which seems to produce a good hit more frequently than any other.

Note: If you're low on life at this point, you can consume the contents of the blue bottle by pointing it to Werner's face in the inventory. This will restore your life points.

The Sprites' Houses

Look For: Green Potion & Dispel Illusion spell

After you've taken care of the scorpion, find the larger toadstool that you can enter, go up the stairs and talk to the green sprite there. The sprite is grateful for your having killed the scorpion, and tells you of a potion that will help you to get big again. He also gives you a Dispel Illusion spell. Don't stay in the house too long, though, for you might regain your normal height. Leave this toadstool and go to another one, identical in

appearance. Bear left to get there. It will have the same interior as the sprite's house, minus the sprite. There's a cabinet near the bed which has a number of green bottles in it. Take the one which the pink dragon icon tells you to, and get out of the toadstool building. Once outside, put the

green bottle over Werner's face (in the inventory) and watch him grow up to his normal size.

Chelhydra's still roaming around the toadstools; if you talk to her again you'll find out how pleased she is by your performance among the sprites. Once you've heard all that she has to say, go ahead to the bridge and walk back to the fountain.

You've shown courage and wisdom, Werner. When it is time for your election and you have on balance avoided needless violence, you may count on my ring.

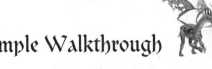

The Fountain Crossroads 4

This time, you'll want to go straight across, to the left path (back to the garden). Among the flowers once more, go to the left and take the path between the red flower patches.

The Cog and the Illusionary Door

Look For: Cog Gap, False Door

You'll come out into a little clearing with a building that has giant gears on its side. Kuru, another Dragon Knight, is pacing around in front of the building. He's not overly fond of the fact that your actions have leaned toward Wisdom, and lets you know that you're altogether too weak for his vote. He'll brandish his sword, but pay no attention to him.

As you face the gears on the building, you'll notice that one of them is missing. The gear in your inventory matches the missing space, so go ahead and put it in. Now, turn to the right until you find the outline of a doorway on the

wall there. Stand in front of the outline, and cast the Dispel Illusion spell. The lines will vanish, and a passageway will be revealed.

The Labyrinth

Look For: Upside-down Bucket, Upside-down Water, Torch

Go straight along the stone hallway until it forks. The path to the right leads to another door, which opens into a room with an upside-down lake.

The path to the left leads to another set of forking hallways, so go ahead and take this one. At the next fork, go to the right, as the left one leads to a door that will not open.

At the end of this hall, take the fork to the left. You'll find a red-floored room with a secret door — ignore that door! There are also a couple of structures in the middle of the room. Take the one closest to you, with an upside-down bucket on the top.

As you return to the hallway, go to your left. (This is the hallway that forked to the right, as you came in.) This will bring you to the white-floored room, where you pick up the torch. You'll meet Klaus von Straupzig here, and he'll give you a talking to. He wants you to crush anything or anyone you meet, spill a lot of blood, that kind of thing. Nice guy, Klaus. Shame about his tail. Leave the white room before he gets a rise out of you. This is one guy you do not want to challenge.

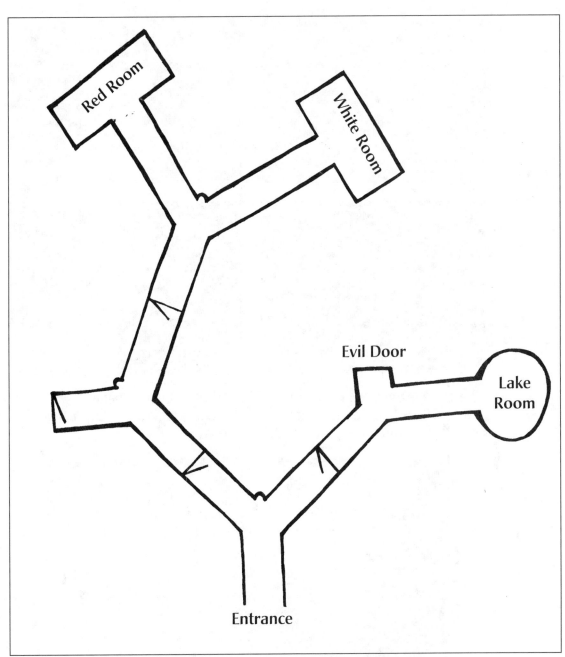

The Labyrinth

And that is when the scales may be tipped towards Strength or Weakness, Power or Pity. Shed blood, boy! Leave a crimson trail and you will earn the vote of Klaus von Straupzig!

As you leave and get back to the choice of hallways, head down to your left. This should bring you back to the original fork. Now, bear left and return to the room with the upside down lake.

Using the Bucket

Look For: Lever

In here, click the bucket to the ceiling and to fill it with water. Go out, take a left down the hallway, and another left to get outside again. Once you're outside, take the bucket full of water and hang it on the lever which you'll find in the top right of the wall with the gears on it. (Click the bucket on the lever.) This action opens the gate to the left.

The Treasure Chest

Look For: Chest

Go through the hallway and up the stairs, into the room with the chests in it. Two chests are balanced on a long plank that acts like a seesaw. Take the chest closest to you and watch the other end of the plank fall. Turn around and go back out, entering the labyrinth again.

Using the Chest and Fujitomo's Ring

Look For: Fujitomo's Ring

 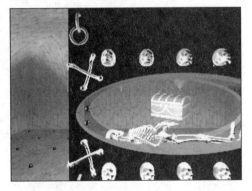

Retrace your steps to the red-floored room, and this time enter the secret door. At the end of the hall there's a crypt room. This elaborate black

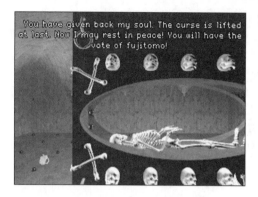

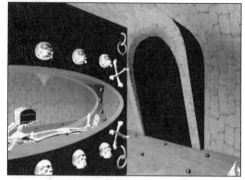

structure is the crypt of Fujitomo, the Dragon Knight whose ring has not yet been claimed. Go around to the right side of the crypt, take the chest from your inventory and place it into the hands of the skeleton.

The crypt will sink down into the ground, and then rise again. Werner steps in to pick up the ring, and the skeleton's spirit speaks, assuring you both the ring and the vote of Fujitomo.

Using the Torch

Behind the crypt is a dark, dark tunnel. Take the torch out of your inventory and left-click it on the center of the dark door to head on in.

Herg's Quest

On the other end, there's this pacing Viking type who urges you to kill the pike. Or let him swallow you. Hmm. Confusing. Could it be a clue? The Viking is Herg nach Drakonen, another Dragon Knight. His deal is simple. There's this Duck Dragon, see, and its furnace melts all of its jewels into one fabulous stone. Buy Herg off with the jewel, or you've lost his vote.

The Pike 1

Look For: Diamond

Take the path opposite the door in the mountain, and you'll reach the river. Click on the water, and oooops, in goes Werner. Sure hope he can swim. That's when the big pike (it's a fish!) comes by and swallows you up. There's a large diamond on the floor of the fish's belly; make sure you pick it up and take it along. This is where the flowers you picked a

while ago come in handy. Take one of the yellow flowers, and click it on the right side of the pike's belly. This tickles the poor creature so much it spits you out — and onto the other bank of the river. Thud.

Waterfall and Duck Dragon

Look For: Waterfall Entrance, Dragon's Jewel

Take a left and go straight ahead, through the rock formations. Walk beyond the willow tree and to the edge of the pool. Go into the pool, and you'll "jump" down to the edge. Then turn to the left and go into the waterfall. When you see the Duck Dragon, choose the diamond from your

inventory and click it on the Duck Dragon to hypnotize him. He'll take it from Werner in a touching animated sequence and then you follow him until he gets between his big stones. The dragon icon will tell you to pick something up, so do so, taking the precious gem the Viking craves. Go back out through the falls, and face the earthen wall to the immediate left of the falls. Click up on the face of the hill, and Werner will get the bright idea to look up and scramble. This brings you back up to the willow tree.

Back to Herg

Go straight ahead until you reach the bank of the river. Face the other side, and jump in again. This time you'll manage to swim to the other side. Hop up, and turn to the left, returning to Herg the Viking. Just click

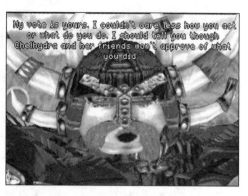

on him with that gem, and he'll wax poetic. The upshot of his ravings is that you'll get his vote, although the Dragon Knights who side with Wisdom won't necessarily like your action.

The Pike 2

Turn around, head back to the river and jump in again. Here comes the pike — once again, you're inside the belly of the giant fish. Go ahead and use your last yellow flower to tickle his ribs — from the inside, of course.

Note: If, for some reason, you failed to collect two of the yellow plants in the garden, you can attack the pike from the inside to get the same effect. Just choose a weapon and start swinging.

Crossing the Water

Look For: Rocks in Water

As the fish spits you out, you'll see Werner perform another beautiful gainer onto the shore. Go left once more to reach the pool near the waterfall. As you face the pool, click to go forward. The screen will move as though you've taken a perilous step, but one click to the left and three rocks will appear in the center of the pool which weren't obvious before.

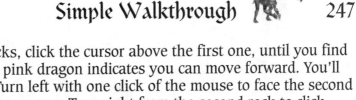
Facing these rocks, click the cursor above the first one, until you find the place where the pink dragon indicates you can move forward. You'll jump to that rock. Turn left with one click of the mouse to face the second rock, and repeat this process. Turn right from the second rock to click above the third. And then a left to click onto the bank. Whew. All that rushing water is a bit nerve-wracking.

The Spiral Path

Go straight ahead through the trees, and you'll reach another stone path, with dolmens off to the right. Keep going straight ahead, until you reach the mountain. When you can't go straight ahead anymore, bear right and you'll see the beginning of the path to the stone citadel off to your right. Head up the stone path under the rock archways. It's a long way up and around . . .

Heleynea

When you click on the rock arch in front of you, a dragon bearing a woman will appear. It lands, and Heleynea descends to come and talk with you. She needs to be convinced that you are in fact Werner von Wallenrod, and the way to let her know this is to show her your ring. Make sure it's the von Wallenrod ring, and not the Fujitomo one. The way to show it to her is to left click on her with the

ring. Not hesitant in the least, the staunch Heleynea then offers you a duel to test your mettle.

We won't break the Pact of Peace, since we're not enemies! Our two families have been allies for many generations. A friendly duel, that's all I'm suggesting. Either of us may end it by throwing down their weapon!

At this point you'll want to arm yourself with any of your weapons, and take a swing at her. Heleynea will hit you a few times. Not a lot of fun, but necessary. After a few smacks — and you may wish to hit her again, too — she decides that you're both honorable and courageous, and promises you her vote. She also heals you, so that your life points (and magic) are

totally restored. Then she gives you a one-shot weapon — a pickax that you can only use once. With that, she's gone. Nothing for you to do but head back down from the citadel. (This can be a little tricky, as you'll have to line the cursor up exactly with the beginning of the stone path that brought you up here. Going all the way to the edge of the citadel, and then some, can help.)

The Avalanche and the Pickax

Return to the original stone road and turn onto the road going left, past the citadel. As you go along on it, you reach a point where it appears to be blocked. This is the result of an avalanche; using the one-shot pickax is the only option you have here. Choose it from your inventory, and click on the blockage with the ax — and voila! It's all clear and time to move forward.

The Gorge (Diakonov and the Tree)

At the muddy stream, you'll find there's apparently no way to cross. The ominous footsteps belong to none other than that king of darkness, Haagen von Diakonov. There's nothing left to do; you'll have to talk to him. He taunts you about your humble origins and casts aspersions on your family, in that sort of warm, personable way he has. Nothing is too low for

this villain; he even stoops to mentioning Daisy the cow. Wait a minute, whose side is this guy on, anyway? Now he gives you an ax to cut down the tree near the stream. And then he's gone. These Dragon Knights, there's no way to be sure . . . they come, they go, they give you axes. . . .

So go and cut down the old tree. You're clearly not as sentimental as your ancestors were. The tree falls across the stream. As you approach the side of the tree, click on it to move forward (watch for the dragon icon to indicate that you can move forward at a particular spot on the trunk).

The Two Thieves

Look For: Kuru's Sword, Staff, Bag (with Vase)

As you walk along through the trees, two thieves will come toward you. The best way to deal with them is not to. Kill them off before they get a

word in edgewise. Then ransack their stolen goods. There are three things to take: a sword (which turns out to belong to Kuru), a staff, and a bag. You can discover the contents of the bag by right clicking on it while it's in your inventory. It turns out to hold two vases — a broken one and a whole one. Throw the broken one away,

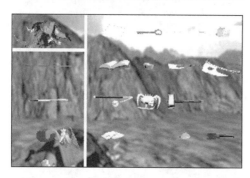

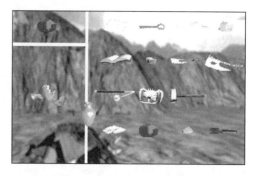

you've got no use for it. The whole vase will come in handy shortly. The bag itself can be used to store other inventory items if you get low on space.

Sylvan and Alexander (the Vase)

Next, go straight ahead through the clearing between the two mountains, and you'll come to a courtyard where you encounter Sylvan and

Alexander, a two-headed, four-armed, four-axed fighting giant. They're both Dragon Knights, and each is willing to give you a vote in exchange for a vase that was stolen by those hapless thieves you slaughtered back at the creek. The dilemma is this: two knights, each wanting a vase. There's only one good vase, as the other one was smashed. Now what? The good news is that it doesn't really matter which one of these clowns you give the vase to — you're only going to get one vote out of these two, anyway, and there's no way for you to win over both of them. No matter which one you give it to, the other will be upset and vote against you. Petty, petty. Tsk, tsk. Oh, well.

As you look ahead in the courtyard, you'll see the castle silhouetted in the distance. (Good time to save your game.) The series of archways in the structure resembling an aqueduct will lead you there. As you walk

through the archways and reach the entrance of the castle, the game will pause itself for an important event — and tell you to *Please insert CD 2*. Once it's in, click the left mouse button to continue.

And enter the gate.

THE CASTLE

Guardian Dragon

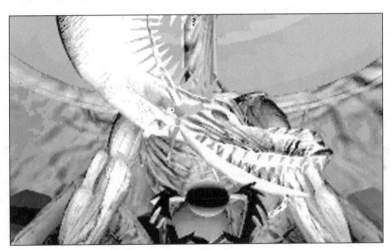

Proceed up the stairs and in the door to meet the most enormous dragon you've yet encountered. Don't be afraid to look into its face; there's an interest sign from your cursor, but there's nothing you can do. Yet. Click on the sphere in front of the dragon to trigger an animation, then go ahead around the figure and between the feet of this dragon.

The Drawbridge

This puts you out onto a drawbridge, leading to another part of the castle. Talk to the green dragon at the end of the drawbridge, and click on

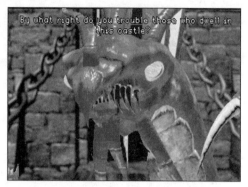

him with your dragon ring to get by. (Before you go in, if you haven't done so already, this is a good time to consolidate the items in your inventory. Putting less necessary items in the bag, like the canteen, the grappling hook, the key to the other tunnel that you didn't take, and the cleaver you took off of Diakonov's ghoul is a good idea. You could also drop them altogether. The choice is yours.)

The Throne Hall (W Room) 1

Enter the great hall. There's a ghoulish fighter roaming around. Take a few steps forward so that he doesn't hem you in against the wall, wait until he gets into range, and then whomp him with your mace. The sideways strokes seem to be the best. Keep moving around to evade his blows. One strategy that works really well is to climb onto one of the sets of stairs under the huge dragon statue's feet, so that you're slightly higher than the ghoul. Then keep bashing him in the head. After about six hits he'll go down, though you might have to chase him around the room to finish him off after you've made a few solid hits.

The Chapel and Vestry

Look For: Bible, Candles, Triangle 1, Holy Water

As you face the W in the middle of the floor, go left along the wall until you reach the stone-arched door on your left. Go in to visit the chapel. Once inside, hang a quick right and walk to the back of the chapel and

take the door on your right, which leads to the vestry. As you enter the door, turn three clicks to the left until you see the book on the lectern in the corner. Pick up the book; as you examine it in the privacy of your inventory, you'll find it is a Bible. Gosh, what a surprise. At the foot of the bed, there's a cabinet that has some

candles on its lower shelf. Take those along as well. Time to go back into the chapel.

Once in the chapel, turn to your left and go all the way up to the altar. Face the altar, and return the candles you picked up in the vestry to the candelabra. The moment you do this, the surface behind the

candelabra will open up, and give you a triangular gold piece. Stow this away in your inventory; you'll need it later. Next, pick up the gold Holy Water sprinkler from the right of the altar (the item that resembles a rattle). At this point, you've collected all you can from here, so make your way back to the W room via the door to the left of the altar.

Cut across the W room diagonally, to the right. Aim for the door on the wall to the right, which appears to be between the feet of the giant dragon statue. The door you want has a small dragon with an arched neck directly to its left.

Rose Bedchamber

As you enter this rose-theme bedchamber, a click or two to the right will bring the fireplace into view. The andiron on the left

triggers your cursor's interest sign, so click on it. Now turn to your left, and go through the archway with the curtain hanging to its right, as well as the next archway, which is covered by a pink curtain.

Chessboard Room

Look For: Key, Triangle 2

In this chessboard room, click on the chandelier above the chessboard. It gives you a key with which to unlock the chest on the floor. As the chest opens, you collect a second gold piece. When you put it into your inventory, click it onto the first gold piece, and the two triangles will form a gold square.

 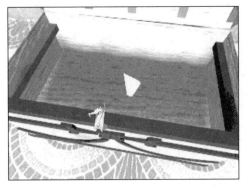

Once you've collected the second gold piece, your adventures in the rose-colored rooms are at an end, so go out the way you came in, back to the main W hall. Now, take the door directly on your right, the one with the tapestry to its left.

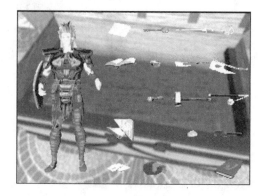

Downstairs

Look For: Sword

You'll see the staircase going up, and hear the wind whistling about. Click to the left, and take the stairs going down. You'll reach a door with a small square on it. Ignore this for now, and click to your right until you see the sword hiding under the stairs. Take the sword, and go upstairs, returning to the main W hall.

W Room Again

Look For: Throne

As you turn to your right, move forward to face the throne on the right hand wall. Click on the serpent on the throne, and Werner will hear a conversation from the past between an agent of Diakonov and Axel von Wallenrod, Werner's father.

The agent, a worm in worm's clothing if ever there were one, tells Axel that he's been sent with a gift from Diakonov, as a symbol of the peace among Dragon Knight families. Axel, obviously a good and noble man, thanks the agent for the splendid gift of a brass serpent — but this serpent comes with blood on its head! The agent

gleefully informs Axel that it is his own (Axel's) blood, taken from the phial he gave, along with each of the other Dragon Knights, to secure peace among the Knights. It is treason, the Pact of Peace is finished and Axel is dead, calling for you to avenge him. Once the sequence is over, the serpent is gone from the throne, and there's no lingering doubt that you will avenge the death of your father.

Room to Left of Throne

Look For: Shield with Missing Sword, Triangle 3

Once this is over, head to the left and enter the door directly to the left of the throne, on the same wall. Between the red curtains just ahead of you, there's a shield with one sword on it. Return the sword you

picked up downstairs to the shield, and it swings aside to let you pick up a third and final gold piece. As you put this one on the other two in your inventory, the combined pieces form the von Wallenrod Family Seal. Go back out to the main W hall, and take the door on your right.

Mustard-Colored Drapes

Look For: Eyeball 1, Effigy

Once inside, click to the right to see two doorways hung with mustard-colored drapes. Go down the hall to the one with the bottles on the floor. Just ahead of you, there's a shelf on the wall with two bottles on it. The one to your left triggers a "Look at this!" reaction from the dragon cursor. Take any weapon you have out of your inventory, and replace the cursor with it, so the weapon isn't in Werner's hand. Then left-click the weapon onto the bottle to break it open. Oh, but that's not all. Click on the broken glass to get a close-up view of the shelf. Amid the fragments of the

broken bottle, you'll see — an eyeball! Eeeeew, that's kinda gross, huh? Be that as it may, you'll pick up that eyeball, and stick it in your inventory for future use. Now, back away from the shelf, and turn around to go back though the hallway.

Hang a right into the smaller room, hung with the mustard-colored drapery, and from above the bed, collect the small figure chained to the wall. Now bail on out of here, down the hallway, and back to the main W hall.

The Library

Look For: Instruction Book

Cut across this room diagonally, again, past the sunlight streaming through the windows on your left, to the far right wall and the small door just to the right of the dragons.

This ransacked library holds many secrets you'll never hear. Click to the left to enter. Isn't that a picture of Chelhydra on the wall in front of you? Advance into the room until you reach the table, then click to the left until you see the dragon sculpture/bookstand to the left. Click on it, and it contains a step-by-step, do-it-yourself approach (complete with illustrations) to freeing caged souls:

"Lay the receptacle in which the victim is trapped, usually a small copy of the victim, before the victim's feet. Then break it with a symbol of Harssk, the man-dragon God. Over the broken receptacle, shake a sprinkler that comes from a holy place."

Downstairs Again

Well, now that you're the wiser for knowing this process, turn around and return to the main W hall. Once in the hall, go to the door that's all the way down at the end, directly in front of you. Ah, back to the stairs. Click left, and go down. Now that you have reconstructed the seal of the von Wallenrod family, you can click the seal onto the square patch on the door.

Sealed Room

You enter a room with a large pink tapestry on the stone wall just ahead of you, and an arched doorway to the right. Advance, and turn to the left. The appetizing sight of an impaled skeleton greets you — get used to it. There's also a door in front of you that you'll want to go through.

Barrel Room

Look For: Ladder, Broken Key

This room has a bunch of barrels, a row of keys, and a ladder in it. Advance and turn to the left, and go up the ladder. Grab the broken key at the top of the shelf, then click on the bottom of your screen to get back down the ladder. Turn around, and exit the way you came in. This time, take the door straight across from you, the one flanked by two small alcoves.

Downstairs Hallway

You enter an enormous hallway, with lots of doors and pillars. Turn to the left, and go into the first door you come to, beneath the chandelier.

Cell Room 1

Look For: Eyeball 2

You're facing a cell-style bed, the kind that prisoners aren't even comfortable on. There's a blanket on the plank; click on it to watch it lift itself off of the plank. Click to the right twice, until you see the open archway with the broken door in front of it. Go on through. Click twice to your right to see another cheery pallet, with a skeletal inhabitant. Click on the skeleton's ribs and it will perform a macabre chiropractic miracle, spinning its head around and presenting you with — another eyeball. Take the eyeball, and add it to your collection. Click twice to the left of the skeleton to find the exit door, and you'll be back in the hallway with the pillars.

Downstairs Hallway Again

Go down the hall until you reach the next door on your left, and head on in. There's a dark gray coat of arms on the wall in front of you. Turn to your right, and take the door at the end of the hall into the kitchen. The sound of flies will inform you that you're in the right place. Whaaack.

The Kitchen

Look For: Ladle

Advance toward the small table in front of you, and pick up the ladle to the left, on the table. Now turn around, admiring the turkey carcass on the block as you do so, and exit the way you entered. Once in the hallway with the coats of arms on its walls, turn to the left and go into the main pillared hall.

Downstairs Hallway Again

Inventory Note: By this time, your inventory is probably way too full, so this is a good place to drop some of the unnecessary items in it. This is a fairly central

space, and it's easy to remember if you need to come and retrieve any of the
objects, but you could drop them anywhere else you choose.

*Suggested items to toss — the halberd, the blue piece of cloth, the canteen, the
cleaver, the grappling hook, and the faerie's key. Now you can put a few more
things in your sack, to make space for some of the other objects you'll be carrying.
The ring of Fujitomo is a good one to put in the sack, to keep you from confusing
it with the von Wallenrod ring in a pinch. Another possibility is to put the soul-
awakening objects, like the Harssk idol, the water sprinkler, etc., into the bag. It's
up to you.*

Cell Room 2

Look For: Eyeball 3

Now that that's done, head out of
the room with the coats of arms
on the walls, and go to the left.
Take the door that's straight
ahead, on the adjacent wall. Ah,
more planks disguised as
servant's quarter beds. Click to the
right, and you'll see that one of
them is broken. There's a door
straight ahead; go through it.

The next room has a water-container contraption with a spigot on it. There's a bowl to the right of this, and another plank bed to the left. Go over to the bed, and click on the blanket. What's this? Another eyeball? Take it along. There's only one more eyeball to find, now. Exit through the arched door directly behind you (not the one through which you entered), to the right of the spigot contraption. Now turn to the left and proceed down the hallway until you reach the door on the left.

Forge Room

Look For: Coal, Bellows, Hammer, Water Trough, Hacksaw

You'll enter a room that, for a moment, looks exactly like the one you just came from (due to the number of pillars around), but don't be fooled. This is the smithy, and as you click to the right, you'll see that you have a lot of work to do in here. After all, you've got a broken key to mend. First things first, so you'll need to cross the room at a diagonal, and go into the

door all the way at the back and to the right of the forge room.

Go to the right, and you'll face an enormous woodpile. There's a kind of caged room on your right, with a lot of wood piled up in it. As you enter it, you'll face a ladder going up to some shelves, though you can't go up this ladder. Turn to your right, until you're looking to the right of the woodpile. There's a sack of coal in the corner, just waiting for you to come and get it. Pick it up, and head back to the smithy.

Once in the forge room again, take the sack of coal and click it on the fire-pit. It automatically opens and fills the pit with coal. Now, go into your inventory and make fire by clicking the flint onto the sulfur. Or vice versa. However you do it, you'll make a fire, which goes into the firepit on top of the coal. Next, click on the bellows to increase the flame in the

pit. Once that fire's roaring, take the broken key from your inventory, and click it onto the fire until it turns red. Now place the red-hot key on the anvil, which is that gray block next to the firepit.

Your next move is to go to the table in the corner of the room, the one with a collection of knives and such on it. (Behind the bellows.) Pick the hammer up from the table, and click it onto the red key. The hammer will disappear. Now, cross over to the water-trough, to the right of the table

the hammer came from, and dip your ladle in it until it's full of water. Return to the red key on the anvil, and click on it with the ladleful of

water. Once you've poured the water over the key, the ladle will disappear and the key will be in your cursor's place, whole and new-looking. Go ahead and put the reforged key into your inventory. The final task in the smithy is to pick up that hacksaw near the barrel that sits between the anvil and the other wooden table, if you haven't already done so. Place the hacksaw in your inventory.

Locked Double Doors

Leave the smithy and go down the shallow steps into the lower level of the pillared hall. There's a set of double wooden doors at the lower wall which you cannot pass through. Clicking on these doors with the reforged key, however, will gain you the access you crave.

You come into an underground tunnel. Go to the end of it, then click left until you go down some shallow stairs to face another set of double wooden doors.

The Three-Headed Dragon Room

As you come out on the other side of the tunnel doors, you'll see a gigantic dragon fountain which is dry, above an equally dry pool. Go approximately three clicks to your left and past the massive bricked pillars until you find an arched wooden door back in the left corner. Go through this door to enter the armory.

Armory

Look For: Eyeball 4, Skull Ornaments, Key, Crossbow, Shield, Sword

To your right, there are racks of weapons. To your left, there are four tables with magic glass blocks on them that each have weapons sealed within. Take a couple of steps along the left wall, until you reach the second weapon rack, the one with the maces hanging from it. Look upon the lower shelf, and you'll find the last eyeball. Go back to the door, and face the room again. Advance along the wall on the right of the room, looking for the metal skull with a ring in its mouth. This will be hanging on a pillar to the right. As you face it, you notice that the eye sockets correspond to those eyeballs you've been collecting. Time to retrieve them from your inventory — well, two of the eyeballs, anyway — and restore this skull's vision.

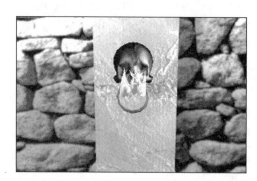

As you turn around, two of the glass blocks have disappeared, leaving behind a key (on the table to the left) and a crossbow (on the

table to the right). The other skull needing its eyeballs is on a pillar similar to the first one, on the opposite side of the room. The table on the left yields you a shield, much better than the one you have now, and another sword. If you try to arm Werner with the shield in the inventory, you'll be in for a disappointment. You will be able to use the sword, however . . . soon.

Torture Chamber

Look For: Pliers

As you come out of the armory, head diagonally across the fountain room, to the door on the far wall which is to the left of the cage-cells. This is the entrance to the torture chamber.

The red-trousered, club-swinging goon who oversees the torture chamber will fall in about four hits from your new sword. Once you kill him, look for the round corner table to the left of the hanging cages. There's a pair of pliers which you'll need to pick up for future use. You may want to stay in here and indulge your sense of the macabre a bit more, by clicking on the implements of torture and watching the resultant animations, but the pliers are all you really came in here to get, so you can bail out as soon as you've got them.

Pool Room

Look For: Crank, Secret Exit

As you return to the fountain room, simply walk straight ahead down to the end of the hall. The door you're facing opens onto a lovely marble wall. Turn right at the wall, and head up the steps. Both flights. You find a pool at the top, lined with marble pillars. Hold your nose, and jump in. Carefully note where you're standing before you do so. The pillars behind you are

separated by wall carvings, which you'll also be able to recognize underwater.

In the far right corner, you'll see a crank on the bottom of the pool (once you're underwater, that is). Ignore the doors; they're of no use until you've drained this pool. Pick up the crank, then turn to the left,

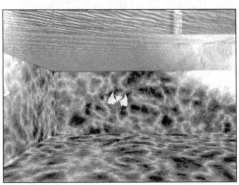

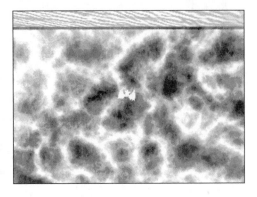

staying along the wall. There are four or so discolored patches on the side of the pool, and the dragon cursor will indicate that you can go ahead even though it appears that you cannot. Click to move ahead, and you'll be back on the marble sides of the pool, on the opposite side from where you entered the pool. Make your way back over to the side with the carvings, and head down the stairs.

Three-Headed Dragon Room (Again)

Look For: Small Dragon Fountain

Upon your return to the fountain room, click to the right to face the fountain, then go around the corner on the right to another, smaller dragon fountain. Click the crank on this dragon, and the water will begin to flow again. Turn to face the central fountain, and go around it to enter the middle cage-cell.

Cells

Look For: Skeleton Effigy, Trapped Soul, Magician's Key

In the middle cell, click on the miniature skeleton that is chained to the wall. You need this to begin the ritual to free the soul of the poor chained skeleton in the next

cell over. Take the effigy to the cell on the right, and click it onto the large skeleton chained to the wall. The small skeleton will disappear. Smash the small effigy by placing the Harssk effigy on it. Next, take the Bible and click it onto the skeleton. It, too, will disappear. Then click on this collection of bones with the Holy Water sprinkler. Click one last time on the skeleton, and the whole thing will disappear. On the floor of its cell there is now a key where the grateful soul has been freed. Pick it up, and you'll discover that it is the Magician's key.

Pool Room (Again)

Back up, out of the cells, and go along the wall down to the end of them, and back into the pool room. The pool is now empty, and you can jump into it to reach the door on the right. This door takes you outside.

Once outside, turn to the right and follow along the path until you reach a small cave entrance on your right. Go on in.

Dragon Room

Look For: Sleeping Potion, Magic Powder, Dragon Lance, Dragon Saddle

Here's another enormous dragon. Disarm yourself if you are armed, for you will want to speak to him. Click on the dragon, and what a surprise! He knows you well. It turns out that this dragon has been imprisoned by magic here, in your very own castle, through the treachery of Haagen von Diakonov. The dragon asks that you restore his manservant's soul to rest, and gives you a powder to help you reach the upper level of the

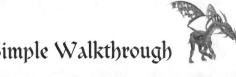

castle. In return, he asks you to return his son to him as a favor. This means getting the molten sphere from that huge dragon you encountered

in that initial room, when you first entered Castle von Wallenrod. Toward that end, the imprisoned dragon gives you a sleeping potion that'll keep that huge guardian dragon sedated while you steal the sphere.

When you're finished talking to the imprisoned dragon, walk around him to reach the door on his other side. You'll pass through the ornate

door into an enormous domed room. The large structure on the left holds a dragon lance and a dragon saddle. Pick them up and take them along. The door at the end of the hall will not open from this side. You have to retrace your steps back to the drained pool room. Jump up on the side, using the same method as before.

Fountain Room (Again)

Look For: Locked Door

Go back into the fountain room, hang a right from the door and go around the corner to the little fountain. To its immediate left, there is a staircase leading down to an ornate door. Surprise, surprise. It's the other side of the lance-room door. Use the Magician's key on it to open it permanently. Once that's accomplished, return to the fountain room and visit the last room yet unseen here, the Treasure Room.

The Treasure Room

Look For: Map

To get there, head for the corner door, directly to the right of the cells. You'll enter a stone labyrinth. Just hang a right and you'll see the

entrance door on your left. The only thing of value you can take from the Treasure Room is the map, which is over to the right, on top of a shining chest. It's a pretty clear map, depicting every floor of the castle.

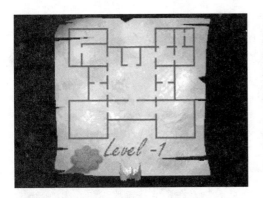 

Up the Stairs

To exit this floor entirely, bear to the left as you return to the fountain room, and go through the double doors. They'll put you back in the earthen tunnel. Go ahead up the stairs, and through the doors at the end. These doors lead back to the pillared hallway. Go through the first door to your immediate left, and you've returned to the room with the pink hanging tapestry. Make a left through the door and go up the stairs. Head back into the main W throne room, and down to the end. Take the door down at the base of the W to head out to the guardian dragon's lair.

Guardian Dragon

Look For: Molten Sphere

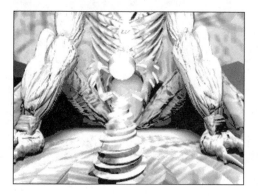 

Click on the dragon's face with the sleeping powder from your inventory. Then click on the molten sphere and bail out of this room, back to the great W hall.

Up the Stairs

Look For: Fog

Head for the door to the right of the throne, and go up the stairs. You'll need to click on the fog that's preventing you from climbing the stairs with the magic powder the dragon gave you. The powder dispels the fog, and up the stairs you go.

In the Nursery

 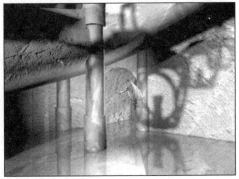

Go through the door at the top of the stairs, and you come into a room with a red rug. Enter the wooden doors at the opposite end of the hall. The doors lead to a marble room with pillars on the left and a red trellis on the right. Head all the way down to the end of this hallway and go through the door on the left, under what is actually a staircase. This door leads you into the nursery. Turn right and go through the door there, to enter a hallway with a yellow-patterned floor.

Egg Room

Look For: Dragon's Egg

Without advancing into the room, turn two clicks to the left, and you'll see the barred window, behind which is a broken Molten Sphere.

Choose the hacksaw from your inventory, and click it on the bars. They will disappear. Now, go into the window with the egg and the sphere. Turn two clicks to your right, so that you can see the balcony on the opposite side of the tower. Step out onto the balcony on your side, and then turn around to look at the egg behind you. Place

the molten sphere in the nest with the egg. Then take the pliers out of your inventory and click on the sphere with them. Click once more on the sphere with the left mouse button, and the hatchling dragon will be at your side. Head back into the nest and out the window, back into the hallway.

Returning to the Dragon Room

Turn right to go through the doors at the end of the hall, retracing your steps through the nursery. Hang a left at the trellis in the nursery, and go through the door there. Get out from underneath the stone staircase, and go all the way down to the end of this corridor to exit through the double doors. Go straight through the room with the red rug, and take the door at the end to go back downstairs. You'll go down two flights of stairs, until you reach the door with the von Wallenrod seal on it. Enter the room with the pink wall hanging again, and go through the door on the right to reach the pillared room.

In the pillared room, go left around the corner and then make a sharp right down the shallow steps, to the doors on that lower level. Pass again through the tunnel, to the fountain room. Facing the fountain, go left to the staircase and down the stairs. Head through the door at the bottom of the stairs to revisit the lance room, and go all the way through it to the door at the end of the hall. In the dragon's lair again, click on the dragon to return the hatchling.

In a moving scene, the dragon is reunited with the newly hatched baby, and is so grateful that he tells you of a secret room, where only you may go. Then he takes you there on his own back.

Secret Room

Look For: Teleportation Spell, Diakonov's Blood

Once in the blustery room, you'll find a spell on the wall. Take it; it's a spell of teleportation. There are a number of vials in the chest in the corner. These contain the blood of the twelve Dragon Knights. Diakonov's is in the top left corner. Pick it up, and be prepared to have your revenge soon. Cast the Teleport spell, and you're shown a

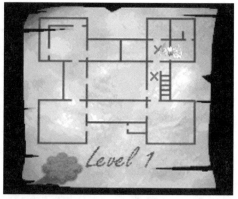

map of the basement with a red X on it. Turn the pages to go somewhere else in the castle, by clicking at the top of your screen. The upper red X on Level 1 is the place to go.

Dining Room

Look For: Skeleton

That X puts you into the room with the red rug on the floor. You see wooden steps up to your right. Take them up. Go through the door into a kind of simple dining room, and there's another skeleton with a halberd. Do not go down the stairs to fight him. Just stay up on the balcony, moving from side to side, and whap at his head until he crumbles. Or, just run past him into the door on the left, avoiding the conflict altogether.

Bedroom

Look For: Metal Ball 1

Go down the stairs into this dining area, and through the door on the left. It opens into a bedroom. Continue to the left, until you reach the small cabinet between the two beds on the far wall. There's a metal ball in the bottom drawer of

this cabinet. Pick it up, turn around, head back into the room with the staircase, and back up through the door on the right.

Marble Staircase Room

Look For: Metal Ball 2

Turn to the left, cross the red rug, and exit via the door at the end of the hall on your left. Back in the marble staircase room, turn sharply to the left until you see the plant at the foot of the staircase. There is another metal ball at the base of the plant. Go ahead and pick it up, then turn to the right and head all the way down the hall, again.

Nursery (Again)

Look For: Metal Ball 3

Take the door on your left to return to the nursery. In the midst of the brightly colored blocks on the floor, to the right, is yet another metal ball.

Note: You could have collected the metal balls earlier, when you were getting the dragon's egg, but there's a danger that your inventory will get too full. The amount of backtracking isn't so great. Suit yourself. Either way works fine.

Getting the Fourth Metal Ball

Look For: Metal Ball 4, Sketch of Fire Phoenix

Now turn to the right and go through the door leading to the yellow-floored hallway, where the dragon egg was before. Down at the end of the hall, there's another door. Open it, and you come out in an enormous yellow-theme bedchamber, where the bed is flanked by two huge dragon sculptures.

Turn right, and take the door out into a hallway whose walls are splashed with light like a sunset. Head through the door all the way down at the end of the hall, and you'll enter another yellow-floored room, only this one's a bedchamber, too. Turn two clicks to the left, and find the final metal ball on the bookshelf. As you turn around, don't exit the way you entered. Not yet.

Go through the door on the farther wall, and it opens into another yellow-floored room with the Roman numerals I, II, III on the wall ahead. This is an obscure hint as to what the balls' action will be. On the table to the right of the numbers, you can click on a scroll that will unfold to

 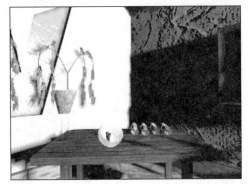

show you another hint — a sketch of the Fire Phoenix.

Now you can turn around, return to the bedchamber where you found the orb, turn left and head out through the doorway to return to the sun-splashed hall. Once in the hall, take the door on your left to enter the formal dining room. This is the site of the Fire Phoenix ritual.

Fire Phoenix Room

Look For: Stick, Fire Phoenix, Four Holes, Talon

Cross the dining room and bear to your left. You'll see the elaborate trunk upon which the phoenix rests, behind a pillar. Go right until you reach the fireplace, and click on the stick that's lying there with the fire. (You can make the fire in your inventory by clicking the flint to the sulfur, or vice versa.) Now you have a torch. Go over to the birdie and click on it with the flaming

stick. Once you've done this, four holes will open in the ground in front of the Fire Phoenix.

Hmm. Four balls, four holes. Coincidence? Probably not. Take one of the metal balls from your inventory and click it over the first black hole

in the ground. The hole and the ball both disappear. Hey, try it again. And again. And one last time, until all of the balls and holes have disappeared. Now, click on the phoenix itself, to watch it display a pyrotechnic moment. Bird flames, door swings open — and you collect the talon which is attached to some string. It was in that case all along. You may have

noticed that there's a key above the bird's head. You can't access it from here, though. Time to exit the dining room, via the door just to the right of the fireplace.

Locked Door on Stairs

This brings you once again to the marble staircase. Go down the hall until you reach the stairs, and head on up to yet another locked door. Well, you can pull out your trusty "2nd Key" from your inventory — remember the one you found on the table in the armory, all those levels ago? Well, whaddya know? It works here, and you go through a

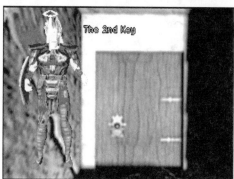

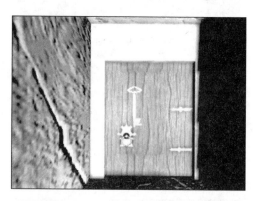

wooden door, only to be attacked by a serious déjà vu as you come face-to-face with another wooden door.

Kettle Room

Look For: Special Kettle, Dragon Key

Go on through it, and find the room with the black kettles in it. As you turn to your left, you'll see that the

second pot from the door has a hole in it. Take a look, then get your talon out. Click the talon on the black hole, and you'll retrieve the key from above the Fire Phoenix' head. Pretty clever, eh? As you hold it over Werner's face, you discover it to be a Dragon Key.

Magician's Room

Look For: Addlepate

Once out of the room with the black pots, turn to your right and go up the stairs. Click the Dragon Key onto the wooden door, and go through it. Once in the wooden room with the barrels, click a few times to the left to enter the magician Addlepate's humble

abode. If you are armed at this point, disarm yourself immediately, before you chat with the magician. He's liable to take the sight of weapons in your hand as an unfriendly gesture.

Talk to Addlepate, for he's your biggest ally and he's deeply apologetic. He tells you that he served your father, albeit in a lame way. He knew that Diakonov would violate the Pact, but wasn't sure how to stop him. Addlepate, too, is a prisoner of Diakonov's magic. Finally, he answers the question that's been annoying you throughout this entire quest — why were you, a von Wallenrod, living in squalor with a surly farmer? Oh, yes. A traditional lesson in humility.

Addlepate is also a great source of information about Diakonov's malevolence. He tells you that there are obstacles in your way — as if you hadn't noticed by now — which have been engineered by Diakonov, and that even if you manage to call out the Dragon Knights, you may not win a majority of votes. Even after all the trouble you've been through. In fact, to further complicate your quest, it turns out that you can't even call out the Knights without wearing the Dragon Armor.

Always an optimist, Addlepate sends you up to the top of the tower, to find the way to open your father's crypt. He asks that you put the weapons you've found in the armory on the floor in front of him, so that he may make some magical blessing over them. Unless you do this, you won't be able to go up into the tower, so step out of the room for good luck, and step back in to lay the goods — the sword, the shield, and the crossbow — at his feet.

He mumbles a few obscure words over your weaponry, and tells you to pick them up again, but you can't do so for some reason, to be revealed later.

The Tower

Look For: Ladder, Ruby

Go ahead to the archway behind Addlepate and through it to the tower entrance. Through the door and up the stairs with you, and you'll come out onto a turret. Walk around the wall until you reach the arched door. Go in, and climb up the ladder to the very top of the tower.

A ruby is hidden to the side of one of the pillars just across from the opening of the ladder. Once you've got the ruby, back down the ladder. Literally. Then out onto the parapet and return to the wooden tower door, which takes you back to Addlepate.

Magician's Room (again)

As you talk to him again, Addlepate promises you a map of the region. He also reminds you to wear the Dragon Armor before calling for an election. Since he's obviously not going to divulge anything more at this time, you may as well go outside his room and cast the Teleport spell. Flip through the maps of each level in

the castle until you reach the magic area map that Addlepate, helpful magician that he is, just gave you.

Back to the Crypt Room

Look For: Ruby Hole, Dragon Armor, Dragon Shield

Click on the front of the Dolmens on the map, and you'll be dropped back into the skull, in the crypt room. Once there, don't bother chatting with the friendly green dragon you met before; just walk around your father's casket and put the ruby onto the matching hole on the opposite side. Then, walk around the front of the casket and click on the first ruby to open it.

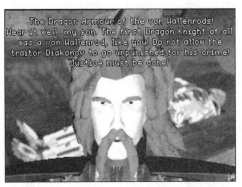

And in a Hamlet moment, you're face-to-face with the ghost of your dear old dad! Axel reappears to tell you about the von Wallenrod armor, and to demand that you punish the wicked Diakonov in the name of justice. Once he's gone, click on the armor, taking it into your inventory, and put it on Werner. (You must take his leather armor off to do

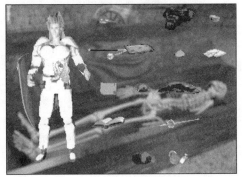

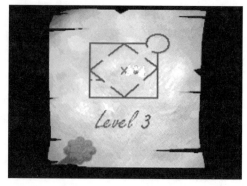

this.) Do the same with the shield, replacing Werner's older shield with this one. Once you back away from the casket, it will close. With the Spell Book in your hand, right click your mouse and you should see the magic symbols on your screen. Use your Teleport spell to return to the castle. Go to the page labeled Level 3 in the book and click on the red X.

Magician's Room (again)

Look For: Chalice & Amulet, Dragon Effigy, Crystal Ball

Once you're back with Addlepate again, he informs you that you must arrive ar the election upon the back of your dragon. Unfortunately, your dragon is imprisoned in the basement, as you probably recall. Addlepate can cast a spell to free the dragon, but he's missing one key component — some of the blood of Haagen von Diakonov. And you just happen to have a vial of it in your possession. Go ahead and try to give it to Addlepate by left clicking on him with the vial.

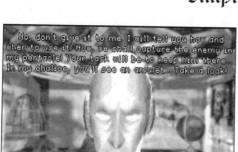

The magician tells you that there's a particular time to use that blood. It's not right now, but he'll tell you when the moment arrives. He gives you a chalice and asks you to find the amulet in it, which you are to throw at Diakonov as Addlepate asks him, "Leaving so soon?" He casts a spell — and the time has come to toss the blood

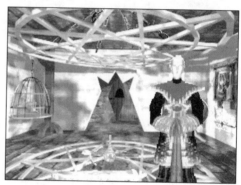

into the pentacle. Left click it somewhere in the pentacle, and who should appear but that taunting villain, Haagen von Diakonov. . .

It looks like there's about to be an intense scene between the two magicians — and it's up to you to make sure that Diakonov loses any power struggles. That's when Addlepate gives you the cue — "Leaving so soon?" And you're staring right into the angry red eyes of your archenemy, Diakonov. Select your inventory, and with the right mouse button click on the chalice that Addlepate gave you. This will open the

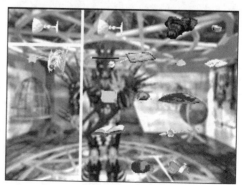

chalice's inventory (the way you previously opened the sack inventory) and you'll find the amulet inside. Select it, right click to close the chalice's inventory, then right click again to return to the action with Diakonov — and touch him (left click) with the amulet.

Diakonov finds it highly amusing that you've attacked him with the source of old Addlepate's power. Addlepate has calmly given his own life in order to trap Diakonov in this pentacle. He forces the captive Diakonov to admit to having killed your father, Axel, and then tells him to drop the von Wallenrod dragon effigy if he wants to be released from this place before Addlepate dies. Diakonov grudgingly complies with this, um,

request, and you get the effigy as Addlepate utters a few more magic words, honorably releasing ol' Haagen. Amid taunts from Diakonov, Addlepate tells you to break the dragon effigy, and to take the crystal ball he gives you. He assures you that you will have your revenge and then he quietly vanishes forever.

If you need to, you can at this point collect your items from the floor, where they've been all this time. If you've fought a vicious game thus far, you may in particular wish to pick up the sword. The shield and the crossbow may not be as significant. If your game has stayed in the Wisdom side of the meter, you probably won't need any of these weapons.

Dragon Room

Look For: Dragon

As you leave the magician's room, you can either make your way back though the castle until you return to the dragon's lair, or you can teleport yourself there by using the spell. (If you use the spell, turn all of the pages in the book until you reach the Dragon's Lair page. Click on the red X to reach it, and fasten your seat belt.)

However you reach the lair, when you see the dragon, you'll need to drop the dragon effigy on the ground and then click on it with any weapon from your inventory to break it and the spell that is imprisoning your dragon. Now that you've freed him, it's time to saddle up this ride and head over to the Dolmens. Take the dragon saddle out of your inventory, and click on the dragon with it. Left click on the dragon and away you go. . . .

SEATS OF JUDGMENT

Once in the Dolmens, Haagen is right in your face, as obnoxious as ever. He starts off the election by voting against you (as if this is shocking to anyone, least of all to you). He reluctantly acknowledges that you have the ring of Fujitomo, and that this is a vote in your favor. Then he calls upon the other Dragon Knights to hear their votes.

If you've played a fairly wise game thus far, the following knights will vote in your favor:

Arthus of Arwyndyll

Herg nach Drakhonen

Chelhydra of Balgair

Helleynea D'Artica

Chen Lai

Fomar Thain

Sylvan of Sygill

(depending on which of the two got the vase)

These knights, on the other hand, will have voted against:

Tanathya Hymenapth

Klaus von Straupzig

Kuru

Alexander of Egregalion

(again, depending on which of the two got the vase)

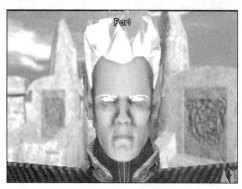

When the results of the voting are in your favor (and if you followed this walkthrough accurately, you should have at least seven positives), Diakonov will acknowledge that you have joined the Dragon Knights. It clearly hurts

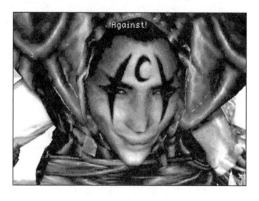

him to have to make this declaration, and he lashes out at your farming background in his usual suave, sarcastic fashion. Helleynea, upset that Diakonov is still cruel to you, stands up for you

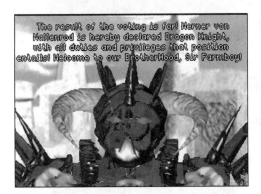

— thereby depriving you of any direct conflict with Diakonov. She's awfully noble, in an interfering kind of way, and exposes his treachery, once and for all.

With Diakonov banished, his lands and titles yours, and your rightful status of Dragon Knight well-earned and restored, you have little to do now but to fly off into

the sunset on the back of your dragon and enjoy the view. He takes you on a tour of the lands you have visited and the locations which were the sites of your many adventures . . . and finally back to your own rightful home, the Castle von Wallenrod. May you relish your triumph and prosper in peace, along with your fellow Dragon Knights.

Other Strategies

Other Strategies

If you've tired of playing Werner as the good guy, and wondered what'll happen if you pursue the route of sheer violence — here are some helpful tips.

The Violent Path

In order to win at a Violent game, you must kill at least two of the Wise Dragon Knights. This way, no majority of peace-loving, disappointed Dragon Knights will be left to vote against you. Chen Lai and Formar Thain are fairly easy to defeat, using the same hit and run away techniques described elsewhere in this guide. Keep swinging your weapon in a rhythmic barrage and they'll go down quickly. This does things to Werner's Force vs. Wisdom rating, so click on Werner's

 face in the inventory screen to see how he fares. Remember, you want the votes of knights like Tanathya, Kuru, and Klaus. You won't get Diakonov's vote no matter what you do.

The choice that you have as a player is to pursue this (violent) path from the beginning of the

game, or to wait until you've made it through the castle and gotten
Addlepate's map. Armed with the Teleport spell and the map, you can
retrace your steps and go back to kill Chen Lai and Formar, or
whoever else you wish. Killing the Sunlit Faerie is a particularly
dastardly act.

    As you play a violent game, you will need the votes of Klaus von
Straupzig, Kuru, Tanathya, Herg nach Drakonen, and either Sylvan or
Alexander. Assuming that you play bloodily enough, and kill off a
couple of the Wise knights, the three Violent knights will give you
their votes without much trouble. It is also advisable to get the ring of
Fujitomo. Though Heleynea is a good friend of the family, her vote is
not guaranteed.

The Killing Spree

Another interesting twist on this alternative is to go back, once you're
on the verge of completing the game, and just kill everyone in your
path (except the knights from whom you want to win votes). This is a
choice for the truly bloodthirsty. Both faeries, your adopted father,

some Dragon Knights, the dogs, tavernkeepers (George and Albert), the dragon guarding the tomb; pretty much anyone who crosses your path can be considered fair game for slaughter.

Note: When attacked, the magical characters (faeries, Addlepate, the guardian dragon, etc.) will cast nasty spells at you. Be prepared to dodge or block them. In most cases, just swinging your weapon repeatedly will suffice.

The Triple Morning Star

Instead of obtaining Fujitomo's Ring, you can choose to use the key the bad faerie gave you and get the chest on the opposite side of the

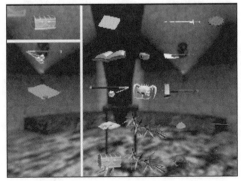

balanced plank (which seems to be a symbol for the balance of Wisdom and Force). The other chest contains a very powerful weapon — the Triple Morning Star — as well as a scroll containing the Poison Cloud spell. It is, technically, possible to win if you make this choice, and the Triple Morning Star drops most enemies with deadly efficiency. However, you will have to discover whom to kill and whom to leave alive. The Dragon Knights vote based on their own private value systems. You can keep the votes of some knights if you are a little violent, but not too much. If you want to try this very tricky route, we wish you good luck. It's an extra challenge to figure out how to get enough votes when you don't have Fujitomo's Ring.

General Tips

Weapons

▼   Some weapons, although not entirely useful in a conventional

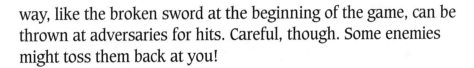
way, like the broken sword at the beginning of the game, can be thrown at adversaries for hits. Careful, though. Some enemies might toss them back at you!

▼ The best weapon during the majority of the game is the Morning Star, or mace, that Werner receives from the tavernkeepers. It has a longer reach than most weapons, which means you can start swinging before your enemy has come within range to strike. When using the hit-and-run fighting technique, this is a great advantage. Once you have the Morning Star, the other weapons are irrelevant.

▼ Using the Dark Faerie's key to collect the Triple Morning Star from the plank in the Labyrinth gives the player a great weapon advantage. Unfortunately, the choice to obtain this weapon means that the Ring of Fujitomo (and the vote thereof) is lost (see Triple Morning Star above for more).

Combat

▼ In combat against any enemy, be it person or creature, the same basic tactic applies: strike at your adversary, hopefully hitting them, and then run a few clicks away, turn, and strike again. Keep repeating this until the fiend has fallen. In this way, you often get in a hit or two, while your opponent cannot reach you.

▼ Also, keep up a rhythmic and constant attack. Usually, if your timing is good, this will prevent your opponent from getting in any hits. This is especially important if you don't have room for the hit-and-run technique.

Beware!

Here are a few things to watch out for:

▼ When trying to talk to a character, you always want to make sure that you are not only disarmed but also free of any items in your hand. Even if you do so accidentally, tossing an item at a character while you are trying to talk to them will usually be interpreted as an offensive gesture, no matter how small and insignificant the item thrown. You'll quickly find yourself in a combat situation that you didn't anticipate. Worse, you might make an enemy of someone whose vote you require. If this does happen, run to another area. When you come back, the person may have forgiven you.

▼ In the castle, on Level 0, there is a sword leaning against the wall in one of the cell cages. Do not touch it, under any circumstances (unless you're in the mood for some superfluous combat)! It triggers a large, fierce spherical enemy to appear, every time it is touched.

What I ask is very simple, master. There is a balcony on this floor, a blaoony that is an nest for dragon's eggs! Tke me there and put me down beside the egg.

▼ In the castle, on Level 1, there is a small stone figure on a balcony outside a window. The figure talks to you and tries to convince you to take it along with you. Don't do it. If you're inclined to take the golem along, at least don't accede to its request to put it in the nest with the dragon egg. It will eat the egg, thereby destroying your destiny with a couple of chomps.

▼ Be especially careful not to attack Addlepate, unless you have saved your game and just want to see what happens. His magic is powerful, and Werner will die in no time flat. It's cool, though.

▼ Finally, there are some spells not mentioned in the walkthroughs. Werner can obtain these spells by searching monsters he's defeated. These include the Lightning Bolt and the Heal Me spells. Neither is really necessary to complete the game, however.

Weapon & Armor Stats

On the following page is a list of weapons and armor found in Dragon Lore and their relative strengths. Some weapons listed here are those wielded by other characters in the game and may or may not be obtainable by Werner. (Weapons are rated on a scale of 0-255.)

Weapon	Rating
Curved Sword	5
Short Sword	10
Morning Star	15
Triple Morning Star	100
Double-Headed Ax	30
Moon Mace	10
Sun Mace	10
War Hammer	5
Neptune Mace	5
Knife	10
Dagger	20
Chelhydra's Sword	20
Heleynea's Sword	10
Kuru's Sword	20
Sprite Sword	15
Chen Lai's Sword	20
Formar's Sword	10
Cleaver	10
Halberd	25
Diakonv's Ax	20
Two-Horned Club	50
Club	30
Spiked Club	25
Quarter Staff	20
Claw Gauntlet	50

Armor	Rating
Leather Armor	5
Wooden Shield	5
von Wallenrod Armor	10
von Wallenrod Shield	10

COMPUTER GAME BOOKS

The 7th Guest: The Official Strategy Guide	$19.95
Aces Over Europe: The Official Strategy Guide	$19.95
Aegis: Guardian of the Fleet—The Official Strategy Guide	$19.95
Alone in the Dark: The Official Strategy Guide	$19.95
Betrayal at Krondor: The Official Strategy Guide	$19.95
CD-ROM Games Secrets, Volume 1	$19.95
Computer Adventure Games Secrets	$19.95
DOOM Battlebook	$14.95
DOOM II: The Official Strategy Guide	$19.95
Dracula Unleashed: The Official Strategy Guide & Novel	$19.95
Front Page Sports Baseball '94: The Official Playbook	$19.95
Harpoon II: The Official Strategy Guide	$19.95
Lemmings: The Official Companion (with disk)	$24.95
Master of Orion: The Official Strategy Guide	$19.95
Microsoft Flight Simulator: The Official Strategy Guide	$19.95
Microsoft Golf: The Official Strategy Guide	$19.95
Microsoft Space Simulator: The Official Strategy Guide	$19.95
Might and Magic Compendium:	
The Authorized Strategy Guide for Games I, II, III, and IV	$19.95
Myst: The Official Strategy Guide	$19.95
Outpost: The Official Strategy Guide	$19.95
Pagan: Ultima VIII—The Ultimate Strategy Guide	$19.95
Prince of Persia: The Official Strategy Guide	$19.95
Quest for Glory: The Authorized Strategy Guide	$19.95
Rebel Assault: The Official Insider's Guide	$19.95
Return to Zork Adventurer's Guide	$14.95
Shadow of the Comet: The Official Strategy Guide	$19.95
Sherlock Holmes, Consulting Detective: The Unauthorized Strategy Guide	$19.95
Sid Meier's Civilization, or Rome on 640K a Day	$19.95
Sid Meier's Colonization: The Official Strategy Guide	$19.95
SimCity 2000: Power, Politics, and Planning	$19.95
SimEarth: The Official Strategy Guide	$19.95
SimFarm Almanac: The Official Guide to SimFarm	$19.95
SimLife: The Official Strategy Guide	$19.95
SSN-21 Seawolf: The Official Strategy Guide	$19.95
Strike Commander: The Official Strategy Guide and Flight School	$19.95
Stunt Island: The Official Strategy Guide	$19.95
SubWar 2050: The Official Strategy Guide	$19.95
TIE Fighter: The Official Strategy Guide	$19.95
Ultima: The Avatar Adventures	$19.95
Ultima VII and Underworld: More Avatar Adventures	$19.95
Under a Killing Moon: The Official Strategy Guide	$19.95
Wing Commander I and II: The Ultimate Strategy Guide	$19.95
X-COM UFO Defense: The Official Strategy Guide	$19.95
X-Wing: The Official Strategy Guide	$19.95

VIDEO GAME BOOKS

Behind the Scenes at Sega: The Making of a Video Game	$14.95
Breath of Fire Authorized Game Secrets	$14.95
Complete Final Fantasy III Forbidden Game Secrets	$14.95
EA SPORTS Official Power Play Guide	$12.95
Earthworm Jim Official Game Secrets	$12.95
The Legend of Zelda: A Link to the Past—Game Secrets	$12.95
Lord of the Rings Official Game Secrets	$12.95
Maximum Carnage Official Game Secrets	$9.95
Mega Man X Official Game Secrets	$14.95
Mortal Kombat II Official Power Play Guide	$9.95
GamePro Presents: Nintendo Games Secrets Greatest Tips	$11.95
Nintendo Games Secrets, Volumes 1, 2, 3, and 4	$11.95 each
Parent's Guide to Video Games	$12.95
Secret of Mana Official Game Secrets	$14.95
Sega CD Official Game Secrets	$12.95
GamePro Presents: Sega Genesis Games Secrets Greatest Tips, Second Edition	$12.95
Official Sega Genesis Power Tips Book, Volumes 2, and 3	$14.95 each
Sega Genesis Secrets, Volume 4	$12.95
Sega Genesis and Sega CD Secrets, Volume 5	$12.95
Sega Genesis Secrets, Volume 6	$12.95
Sonic 3 Official Play Guide	$12.95
Super Empire Strikes Back Official Game Secrets	$12.95
Super Mario World Game Secrets	$12.95
Super Metroid Unauthorized Game Secrets	$14.95
Super NES Games Secrets, Volumes 2, and 3	$11.95 each
Super NES Games Secrets, Volumes 4 and 5	$12.95 each
GamePro Presents: Super NES Games Secrets Greatest Tips	$11.95
Super NES Games Unauthorized Power Tips Guide, Volumes 1 and 2	$14.95 each
Super Star Wars Official Game Secrets	$12.95
TurboGrafx-16 and TurboExpress Secrets, Volume 1	$9.95
Urban Strike Official Power Play Guide, with Desert Strike & Jungle Strike	$12.95
Virtual Bart Official Game Secrets	$12.95

TO ORDER BOOKS

Please send me the following items:

Quantity	Title	Unit Price	Total
_____	_____	$_____	$_____
_____	_____	$_____	$_____
_____	_____	$_____	$_____
_____	_____	$_____	$_____
_____	_____	$_____	$_____
_____	_____	$_____	$_____
	Subtotal		$_____
	7.25% SALES TAX (CALIFORNIA ONLY)		$_____
	SHIPPING AND HANDLING*		$_____
	TOTAL ORDER		$_____

By telephone: With Visa or MC, call 1-916-632-4400. Mon.–Fri. 9–4 PST. By mail: Just fill out the information below and send with your remittance to:

PRIMA PUBLISHING
P.O. Box 1260BK
Rocklin, CA 95677-1260

Satisfaction unconditionally guaranteed

Name_____

Address_____

City_____ State_____ Zip_____

Visa / MC#_____Exp._____

Signature_____

*$4.00 shipping and handling charge for the first book, and 50¢ for each additional book.